W9-BCT-943

The Democratic Experience

Past and Prospects

Reinhold Niebuhr
and
Paul E. Sigmund

FREDERICK A. PRAEGER, *Publishers*
New York • Washington • London

WINGATE COLLEGE LIBRARY.
WINGATE, N. C.

FREDERICK A. PRAEGER, PUBLISHERS
111 Fourth Avenue, New York, N.Y. 10003, U.S.A.
5, Cromwell Place, London S.W.7, England

Published in the United States of America in 1969
by Frederick A. Praeger, Inc., Publishers

© 1969 by Frederick A. Praeger, Inc.

All rights reserved

Library of Congress Catalog Card Number: 68–12711

Printed in the United States of America

INTRODUCTION

THIS BOOK developed out of a course the co-authors taught jointly at Harvard University several years ago. One of the themes discussed in the course was the lack of success of democratic politics in the newly emerging nations, and subsequently the authors set about to look more deeply into the reasons for the relative rarity of constitutional democracy among the new states of Asia and Africa and the older polities of Latin America.

Reinhold Niebuhr begins this study with an account of the rise of free government in the West, isolating what seem to be the factors that have contributed to the (not unmixed) success of that form of government in Europe—the development of national unity, the emergence of individualism, and the establish-

42699

ment of an internal balance of forces that have made government by conciliation both necessary and possible. Then, working with Dr. Niebuhr's outline, Paul Sigmund has drawn on his personal acquaintance with the developing areas to show where the elements are or are not present that encourage the growth and persistence of free government in Asia, Africa, and Latin America.

Both authors have been guided by the belief that democracy is neither a universal panacea nor, at the other extreme, merely a cultural monopoly of the Anglo-Saxon and Scandinavian world. While our study stresses the difficulties in the way of viable democracy, it is also not optimistic about the prospects and performance of alternative forms of government. To put it in Winston Churchill's words, we believe that democracy is the worst form of government on earth except for all others ever tried.

While this study was being written, this pessimistic faith in the democratic idea has been confirmed in a number of ways. The military and one-party states predominant in Asia, Africa, and Latin America have not shown themselves to be superior in the promotion of economic development or political stability to those based on constitutional democracy. The Communist world has been shaken by demands for freedom of expression and domestic and international pluralism. And as this book is going to press, young people in many Western countries are calling for greater participation and more meaningful democracy.

In the United States, we are conscious, as we were not a few years ago, how difficult it is for democratic politics to deal with the problem of race, especially when it is reinforced by economic handicaps. We are aware, as perhaps we were not earlier, that constitutional democracy, if it is to survive, must demonstrate that it can successfully deal with the problems of social justice, economic opportunity, and international peace. The problems of democracy in the more developed nations thus do not seem so different from those in the less developed parts of the world.

As the final chapter indicates, our concern with the problems of democracy in the contemporary world is shared by many other contemporary scholars. It is in the hope that this kind of interpretive essay may aid the policy-makers, the thinkers, and the ordinary citizens who are interested in the survival and development of the democratic ideal that this study is presented.

Our thanks are due to The Rockefeller Foundation for its financial support; to its vice-president Kenneth Thompson for his assistance and encouragement; to our students, whose enthusiasm and interest encouraged us to take a fresh look at an old problem; and especially to our wives, whose support and constructive criticism helped us to bring this collaborative enterprise to fruition.

REINHOLD NIEBUHR
PAUL E. SIGMUND

CONTENTS

I

The Democratic Experience
in Western History

DEMOCRACY AND COMMUNISM: TWO UTOPIAN IDEOLOGIES

A FTER THE END OF World War II, two nations, the United States and the Soviet Union, achieved hegemony in their respective blocs of nations by reason of the imperial scope of their economic and military power and their arsenal of the dreaded nuclear weapons. Both nations also were armed with the political prestige of the typical or ideal embodiment of the prevailing ideology of their respective blocs.

The U.S.S.R.'s prestige derived from the fact that a new Communist religio-political dogma, ambitious to achieve world-wide relevance, had taken root in Russia, where a traditional culture had collapsed under the strain of World War I. It became the holy land of a new culture with pretensions of possessing a cure for all social evils in the revolutionary socialization of "the means of production." This cure had been designed by Marx for what he believed to be the impending crisis of European indus- trialism, a crisis allegedly due to the accentuation of the injus- tices of agrarian feudalism by the new wealth of modern industry. The discrepancy between wealth and poverty would, according to the Marxist apocalypse, ultimately drive the im- poverished workers into revolutionary desperation.

The history of democracy's encounter with industrialism in nineteenth-century Europe has refuted the Marxist apocalypse. The bourgeois democracies did not turn out to be mere stooges of the capitalist class, and modern industry did not accentuate the disparities between rich and poor. Instead, modern technical cultures created a complex class structure that proved amenable to free institutions. The equilibrium of political power, resulting from the extension of the right of suffrage, and the equilibrium of economic power, established when the traditional cultures of Europe and the bourgeois culture of America reluctantly per- mitted the industrial workers to bargain collectively, enabled the laborers to overcome their individual impotence vis-à-vis the owners of industry and to achieve a more equitable share of political and economic power.

A century was required to achieve this triumph over the early injustices of modern industry. This victory made the open socie- ties of the West immune to the virus of the Marxist rebellion, and thus they became the hard core of the non-Communist world. Perhaps this ironic development was responsible for iden- tifying the non-Communist cause with the "West," but the label was inaccurate, because it included neither Japan, Asia's indus- trial nation, nor nonindustrial India, with its democratic ideals inherited from its former British overlords.

On the other hand, the Marxist apocalypse, intended for Europe's industrial culture, found a degree of realization because of the collapse of two traditional feudal cultures, first in Russia and then in China. Lenin's amendment of Marxist dogma, "Soviet power plus electrification," meant that Communism was to become the agent of industrialization—through Stalin's rigorous collectivization of the peasants, which made them impotent to resist the Communist power monopoly when it extracted the capital investment for industry out of their poverty—an ironic refutation of the utopian hope of making the poor rich in the classless society of the future.

Just before the Communist victory in Russia, Lenin, still in Switzerland, wrote the book *Imperialism, the Highest Stage of Capitalism*. In it, he expressed the utopian notions of Marxism but also made the new religio-political movement seem relevant to all the colonial and ex-colonial nations that had suffered or were suffering under European imperial domination. But the idea that imperialism was nothing but the collective expression of capitalist acquisitiveness also served to cumulate all the utopian errors of Marxism. Instead of analyzing the causes of domination as a mixture of exploitative—i.e., economic—motives, the more basic will to power, and the "missionary" wish to export a cause that transcends the nation, whether it be Communism, democracy, Christianity, or even civilization itself, it placed its emphasis on purely economic factors.

To this error must be added two other basic miscalculations of Marx. He inherited from classical liberalism the idea of the supremacy of economic over political power, and he compounded this error by equating the ownership of property with economic power. The managerial economic system that developed in both Communist and capitalist cultures revealed that the power of the manager over the economic process is greater than the power of ownership, whether it be by a private concern or the government.

The hostility that developed between Russia and China after the original friendship between these two nations, both of which had become Communist after their traditional feudalism had collapsed, refuted the utopianism of their common creed. China did, indeed, suffer from resentment after the nineteenth-century humiliations at the hands of European nations. It was thus ripe for the anti-imperialist stance of Communism. But, instead of manifesting the "fraternal spirit" that the Communist creed ordained for all nations that had eliminated that root of all social evil, private property, China, prompted by its national interests, proceeded to challenge Russia.

This challenge revealed the "missionary motive" of the new convert. China was colored and poor. Russia was not only European; by dint of its rapid industrialization, it also was rich. Its more heinous crime, however, was its nascent partnership with the United States, another nuclear power, aimed at preventing a nuclear holocaust. The charge of revisionism against Russia was thus inevitable. Russia was alleged to be in league with the United States, which was the anti-Christ in the Communist scheme of salvation. The common interest in survival of the two supernations of the nuclear age had overridden the utopianism of Communist dogma. This fact, however, did not prevent China from challenging the Russian authority by offering its interpretation of the common faith and, in effect, claiming to be the "Old Believers," the more rigorous exponents and exporters of the revolution that was an article in their common creed.

If political life were purely rational, the Sino-Soviet dispute would put an end to the pretensions of Communism as a scheme of social salvation. Unfortunately, it is a semirational way of manipulating collective irrationalities. Hence, we are confronted not with the atrophy of the Communist creed but with two different bearers of the same utopian scheme.

Furthermore, the non-Communist world, with the United States as the hegemonous power, adds to the irrationality in two ways. First, it immodestly affirms that all non-Communist nations belong to the "Free World," even if that world encompasses South Africa with its modern form of slavery and Latin American nations in which democracy has been superimposed on a feudalism with Spanish-Indian racial overtones. Many of these nations alternate between pseudo-democracy and military dictatorships or dictatorships of the Left, *à la* Vargas in Brazil, Nkrumah in Ghana, and Perón in Argentina. "Democracy" is thus a false claim in many of these nations, as false as Communist pretensions to having established "people's democracies."

Second, our penchant for utopian versions of democracy concentrates too strongly on the relationship of democracy to individual freedom. We constantly extol liberty as if it were an absolute value without reference to either community or justice. We should know that self-government really derives its authority from the moral prestige of a united community. The European democracies could come into being only because predemocratic eras bestowed upon them the necessary unity of race, language, and religion. As a new nation on a virgin continent, we have tended to ignore the services rendered to the unity of the community by predemocratic regimes.

But free governments must not only be built on the essential unity of the community; they also must validate themselves as instruments of justice. We have observed that European culture required the whole of the nineteenth century to survive this test in modern industrialism. As a purely bourgeois culture, we were tardy in coming to terms with industrial problems of collective justice. One might have supposed that our triumph in this realm was so recent that we could not possibly forget this dimension of the validation of liberty. Yet our wealth and our expanding frontier eased these adjustments, so that we had no "class struggle" on the European model.

The tendency in America to give a libertarian interpretation of the realities of self-government, to raise incantations to freedom and liberty without considering the effects of freedom on the community, informs the thought of both statesmen and scholars, and of course businessmen, who are strongly addicted to the libertarian creed. Moreover, the libertarian impulse is so strong that statesmen of opposing political creeds, including both those who have used freedom as an instrument of justice and those who have thought that justice would be the inevitable consequence of a market economy, have been equally vocal in extolling freedom and presenting it as a kind of panacea for all social ills.

Thus, General Dwight Eisenhower, after describing the common interests of the Russian and American victorious allies, soon to be the arch adversaries in the "cold war," proceeds to define the differences between them:

> Ideologically, however, they were in diametric opposition; the United States was devoted to a social and political order based upon individual liberty and human dignity; Russia, dedicated to the dictatorship of the proletariat, seemed in Western eyes to be engulfed in a form of statism under the absolute direction of a new man.[1]

In the same volume (p. 477), General Eisenhower gave an even more specific libertarian interpretation of our democracy. He defined the mission of Western democracy in these words:

> We believe individual liberty, rooted in human dignity, is man's greatest treasure. We believe that men, given free expression of their will, prefer freedom and self-dependence to dictatorship and collectivism. From the evidence, it would appear that the Communist leaders also believe this; else why do they attack and attempt to destroy the practice of these concepts?

One might regard this interpretation as a typical conservative expression of a "free society" by a member of a party which has increasingly opposed political intervention in the economic life. But such a party interpretation is refuted by consulting the addresses of another American President, Franklin D. Roosevelt, who did more than any previous American leader to adjust free institutions to the social realities and necessities of an industrial civilization.

In his well known "Four Freedoms" doctrine, expressed in his State of the Union message to Congress on January 6, 1941, Roosevelt, after expounding the two traditional individual free-

---

[1] Dwight D. Eisenhower, *Crusade in Europe* (Garden City, N.Y.: Doubleday, 1948), pp. 457–58.

doms of thought and worship, embodied in the Bill of Rights, elaborated two additional freedoms, "freedom from want" and "freedom from fear," in which he characteristically related the concept of freedom to the social realities of human existence. Yet—uncharacteristically for a statesman renowned for his sober pragmatism—he let his hopes carry him to utopian heights. On freedom from want, Roosevelt said, "Translated in world terms it means economic understandings which will guarantee every nation a healthy peacetime life for its inhabitants everywhere in the world."

Freedom from fear is even more grandly conceived. Roosevelt explained, "Translated in world terms it means a world-wide reduction of armaments to such a point, and in such a thorough fashion, that no nation will be able to commit an act of physical aggression against its neighbors anywhere in the world." The anxieties of the precarious peace of a nuclear age preserved by a "balance of terror" have vividly revealed the utopian character of this exposition of the possibilities of "freedom from fear" by a very unutopian American statesman. Some deep current in the American tradition must undoubtedly account for the persistence of this note in our national life.

The power of utopian interpretations of democratic government is evinced not only by our responsible statesmen but by our political interpretors. Almost every essay in a symposium of essays entitled *The National Purpose* contains a solemn incantation to freedom; and few deal with the difficulties which free societies have faced in Europe and must face in the world.

Thus an eminent political scientist writes:

> In our youth we had a profound sense of national purpose, which we lost over the years of our rise to glory. The American mission that inspired every statesman from Washington through Lincoln called upon us to serve as a testament to freedom, to spread by our example the good news of personal liberty and popular government throughout the world. We did not lose our youthful sense of mission because it was childish or wicked or impossible in its demands upon us, rather because it had to be fulfilled in due course of time or be

cast aside as a youthful extravagance. And it was in fact fulfilled nobly. For all its areas of blighted hope, the world today counts many constitutional democracies, where once it counted only the United States.[2]

This survey of the status of democracy is hardly accurate in this day, after we have emerged victorious from a conflict with one cynical form of totalitarianism and are involved in conflict with another form, which is rooted in utopian illusions. Could it be that the utopianism of the adversary has colored the thoughts of our own wise men and persuaded us that we must counter illusion with illusion?

A businessman contributing to the same symposium is even more extravagant in his estimate of the mission of democracy and our obligation to extend it. He writes: "Through the generations Americans have always thought of themselves as being in the vanguard of freedom. They cherished an image of their country as the citadel of democracy and morality and a living defiance to despotism anywhere."[3]

One suspects that, indeed, these noble sentiments give an accurate account of the American conventionally held "self image." But in that case the self image implies a frighteningly simple estimate of our responsibilities in breathing "defiance to despotism anywhere." Even the picture of the adversary may be inaccurate in the post-Stalin era. The real ideological content of modern Communism is utopian dogmatism, and the power structure based on this dogmatism is a managerial society in which a political party holds a dangerous monopoly of power.

In so far as the power contest has an ideological content, the non-Communist world may be said to oppose the too consistent collectivism of Communism (although its utopian dogmatism may ultimately turn out to be more dangerous to the future of

[2] Clinton Rossiter, "We Must Show the Way to Enduring Peace," *The National Purpose* (*Life* Series) (New York: Holt, Rinehart and Winston, 1960) , p. 83.

[3] David Sarnoff, "Turn the Cold War Tide in America's Favor," *Ibid.*, p. 51.

human communities). But against this collectivism, the non-Communist certainly does not espouse an "individualism" which believes in "self-dependence" and obscures the social substance of human existence, as much as Communism obscures the "value and dignity" of the individual. Free governments have indeed guarded the mystery of the individual's freedom and dignity, rising in transcendence over all political processes and communal ends and goals. But they have also had to come to terms with the social substance of human existence. They have been under the necessity of validating political freedom by triumphing over the confusions created by various subnational and supernational communities of race, language, religion, and economic class. Any incantation to freedom that obscures the problem of these communal diversities which the developed democracies have faced and which the developing democracies must face gives a false view of the encounter between democracy and Communism.

If the West, and particularly America, persists in presenting our cause as concern for the individual in contrast to collectivism, and if we show a lack of concern for the problems of the communities, for their need to establish harmony and create justice, we will be presenting our cause as a contrasting utopia to that of the Communists.

It is well to remember that Communism is a secularized version of the messianism derived from Hebraic and Christian sources and that this messianism is a by-product of the concept of a meaningful history, which is the contribution of a Judeo-Christian culture to the historical dynamism of the Western world. The two by-products of the historical dynamic were utopianism on the one hand and fanaticism on the other hand. Utopianism is the consequence of fleeing from the confusion of cross-purposes in history to an imaginary ideal future of a heaven on earth. Fanaticism is the consequence of ascribing ultimate significance to proximate and historically contingent ends and goals. Utopianism and fanaticism coincide when utopian visions prompt men to assume a sharp division between good and evil forces in history, which will ultimately result in the victory of the good forces. Communism shares both these characteristics of utopianism and fanaticism. It is therefore a final aberration of the Western concept of the meaningfulness of history.

Western civilization approaches the form of historical dynamic expressed in Communism if it separates another theme of the messianic vision which the Judeo-Christian faith has also bequeathed to the West and emphasizes it excessively. That theme is rooted in the religious affirmation of the direct relation of the free and responsible individual to the divine, without mediation of group or community.

The bourgeois period of Western history lent exaggerated emphasis to the value and dignity of the individual, and obscured the fact that every human being must realize himself in a community, whether family, parochial community, nation, or empire. In short, every individual self exhibits two dimensions: the vertical one, in which it transcends its communities and the flux of temporal events and finally itself, and the horizontal dimension of selfhood which corresponds to the social substance of human life.

Naturally, messianism, which projects an ideal fulfillment of all human aspirations, is bound to assume both an ideal fulfillment of human freedom and an ideal fulfillment of a universal and peaceful community. But since these two dimensions are in contrast to each other, and there is no perfect fulfillment of the two dimensions in history, utopianism and messianism are marked by two characteristics. Either, as in the anarchistic pinnacle of the Communist dream, they project an ultimate goal of the state "withering away," or they sharply divide the two ideals of perfect freedom and perfect community. In both the Cromwellian and the French Revolutions there were conflicts between bourgeois individualistic visions of utopia and the more Communistic and egalitarian visions of perfect community.

The consistently libertarian emphasis in the American ideology is thus a part of the bourgeois utopian tradition. In so far as we attempt to give an ideological content to the power struggle with Russia, we interpret the struggle as one between the nations committed to bourgeois liberalism and those in which collective requirements receive a higher priority, an interpretation which is not radically different from the Communist interpretation of the struggle.

A less obvious disadvantage of this interpretation of the ideological struggle is that it obscures a really important difference in the ideological content of the two contestants. The one contestant has developed a new culture, disciplined by tight dogmatic presuppositions drawn from an original messianic and utopian apocalypse; the other, even in his European core, is culturally pluralistic. Because of this pluralism, and as a consequence of his long encounter with political realities, he has dissipated his utopian illusions. His approach to the political order is characterized by a mature empiricism and realism. He knows that there are many forms of power, not merely one. He knows that there must be an equilibrium of social power as a basis of justice, and he has developed a highly complex political organism with many forms of countervailing power. He also knows that the political authority which must establish the order of the community must be one, but that he must triumph over many forms of subnational communities to achieve this wholeness of authority and be able to speak for the whole community.

The real issue is whether the entire political development of the nations of the contemporary world, now drawn into the modern historical dynamic without regard to their previous cultural and economic development, should be subjected to a dogmatic political faith which obscures the complex problems and forces operative on all levels of political and economic life, or whether mankind shall have the opportunity to arrive empirically at solutions of the complex problems of order and justice.

Forswearing a utopian interpretation of our cause has the advantage of preventing disillusion and hysteria if, in the world-wide struggle, some of the nations allied with us do not reveal

WINGATE COLLEGE LIBRARY
WINGATE. N. C.

the resources necessary for the achievement of a healthy democracy. We will not be too disturbed by evidences of inadequate solutions to the problems of the responsible exercise of power. We will know that dictatorships are dangerous and that all irresponsible power creates abuses. But we will also know that in a world of change, governmental experiments are reversible if they are not controlled by a tight dogmatic system. We will also be prepared for the final emancipation from dogma by the historical realities, as the Communist world becomes more deeply divided over the issues of strict dogmatism or a more realistic approach to domestic and international problems.

While it is impossible in terms of political polemics to define the ideology of our cause as "mature empiricism" in contest with dogmatism, the fact that the contest is fatefully taking place on the edge of an abyss of nuclear catastrophe confronts both contestants with such unparalleled perils and promises that it may be wise to identify ourselves, not by political slogans, but in terms which accurately define the political situation. If this should result in a loss of morale among the politically immature adherents of our cause, it would bring about a gain of wisdom among the politically mature. This wisdom is necessary in a situation in which we have the double responsibility of guarding a civilization with a high content of justice against opposing forces of political fanaticism fed by utopian illusions, and of protecting mankind against the peril of nuclear catastrophe.

Naturally, we cannot overcome the second peril without learning to coexist with the Communist world despite its utopianism and its dogmatism. Every method of identifying our cause that will indicate some measure of community across the ideological chasm and that will beguile the adversary from his aberrations is a source of strength to us. If we are sufficiently empirical in our self-identification and develop an amused tolerance in reacting to the aberrations of the adversary, we have a final chance to escape catastrophe. Meanwhile we must trust our cause sufficiently to preserve our morale without the help of utopian slogans.

Our failure to take into consideration the hazards of a free society, which the nations of Europe faced and overcame, tempts the United States to a libertarian democratic dogma which almost parallels the Marxist utopia. It is necessary therefore to recall the problems in the emergence of free governments, not only in Europe, but in our own history as well, in order to be able to recognize the hazards non-European nations are sure to encounter in the process of rapid industrialization and development. Such a sober analysis will tend to correct the utopian and individualistic interpretation of democracy by which American leaders have sought to make free governments competitive with the Communists' utopias.

2

THE HAZARDS OF RACIAL, LINGUISTIC, AND RELIGIOUS PLURALISM

1. *Diversity in Race and Language*

THE MODERN SOVEREIGN NATION has become a universal norm of community. In the late Middle Ages and early modern period, it arose and triumphed over both the supernational communities of church and empire and the subnational communities of tribe and fief. Race and language were the binding or cohesive forces in the rise of the European nations, and a sense of ethnic kinship and a common language constitute the primary forces of cohesion in the new nations. Their power in even the most advanced cultures is a reminder that no amount of political contrivance (such as monarchy or democracy) can negate the effect of these "organic" forces, which act subconsciously and are not amenable to man's reason and conscious will. Of the two, ethnic kinship is a pure force of nature, while language is more malleable and historical. But the two are usually united and between them serve to give the integral community—in modern terms the nation—both a basis of community and a source of differentiation from other communities.

Despite the "natural" or "organic" character of the cohesive forces of race and language, the nation, created by them, was a late rather than early achievement of history. The early history of community moves from tribe to city-state and from city-state to empire. The obvious reason for this chronology is that some cultural artifact was necessary before language could create the modern nation. That artifact was the written, and more importantly, the printed, word. It triumphed over the localized and orally transmitted dialects, and thus gave the larger ethnic community supremacy over smaller kinship groups. The invention of printing in the fifteenth century was one of the most potent causes for the triumph of the nation over supernational and subnational loyalties, the former governed by a bureaucratic elite with a "universal" or "imperial" language (Latin in Western culture and Arabic in the Islamic world), and the latter bound together by local dialects.

It must be noted that the triumph of the nation over these supernational and subnational loyalties required not only the artifact of the printed word but a high degree of literacy, the product and by-product of a system of education. Thus ethnic and linguistic kinship became the binding forces of the new nations only when cultural artifact had transmuted natural or "organic" forces of cohesion.

While this combination of nature and culture was a late development in human history, it is important to note that it preceded the emergence of free governments by centuries. Nations were born before free governments emerged, and one must assume that only the national community was both large and small enough to allow self-government to emerge. The chronological priority of the invention of printing and the diffusion of literacy over the rise of free governments is important. It points to the fact that many new nations are compelled to counter the hazards of tribal loyalties and dialects within the framework of free institutions, while most European nations built free institutions on a predemocratic triumph of the written language over more parochial loyalties of the tribe and dialect.

This fact of history is sufficient to give pause to any inclination to regard democracy as a live option for all nations on all levels of culture. Many of the new nations do not yet have a single written language. Many more, with a single language, have low standards of literacy. Even a great democracy such as India is confronted by the hazards of a multiplicity of written languages and a low standard of literacy in all of them. The new nation of Burma draconically solved the language problem by teaching only the Burmese language in its schools. The price paid for this measure was the disaffection of five or six of its "frontier" tribes, among whom, incidentally, a Communist rebellion against the democratic Burmese Government was first mounted in 1948.

The geographic and historical factors, influential in the cohesion of national communities are frequently not coincidental with the factor of language. Geographic and historical factors ran counter to the factor of language in the history of both England and France. The Norman conquest gave the kingdom of England to a Duke of Normandy. It took a century of wars to absorb the Gaelic minority of Cornwall into the English-speaking nation and to prohibit the use of French in the English courts, thus welding England into a unified English-speaking nation. Scotland was not united with the English nation until James VI of Scotland became James I of England after Queen Elizabeth's death. This dynastic legitimacy both preserved the unbroken line of royal authority and furnished the minimal force of cohesion between the English and Gaelic Scotland.

These predemocratic organizations of larger national communities are significant because they reveal that a "vertical" source of cohesion, furnished in a common loyalty to a monarch, may surmount divisive forces and bring about a national unity which democracy may find it difficult to achieve, since free societies with their horizontal forces of community are more exposed to the dangers of parochial loyalties.

From the vantage point of modern democracies, dynastic legitimacy as a source of community seems utterly irrational. But that merely proves that modern democracies are too Lockean, rationalistic, and voluntaristic to understand that statesmanship must rely primarily on a rational manipulation of the subrational loyalties of men. In the case of Britain, the triumph of the English language over the Gaelic dialects was a growing force of national loyalty. The monarchical framework provided a sphere in which this triumph could take place. It is, after all, not very much more "irrational" than the "natural" forces of cohesion which it displaces.

The trilingual and bilingual nations of European culture such as Switzerland, Belgium, and Canada remind us that linguistic or ethnic diversity need not be an insuperable hazard to the unity or internal security of a nation, not even to a democratic one. Switzerland is, of course, the favored exception to the general rule. One of the oldest of European democracies, its nationhood was established by a union of German-, French-, and Italian-speaking cantons, and the unity of the nation has never been seriously imperiled, though it has had no "vertical" dynastic frame for community.

The two bilingual nations, Belgium and Canada—the one divided between the Flemish language and people and the French-speaking Walloons, and the other divided between the English-language provinces and French-language Quebec—suggest that even highly localized ethnic and language diversities are no insuperable obstacle to national unity even in a democratic nation.

But these diversities are a source of strain in the community. Thus language-riots occurred in Belgium at the University of Louvain, a bilingual university in the Flemish part of Belgium, and as a by-product of the political animosities consequent upon the loss of the Belgian Congo. In Canada the politics of the nation has always dealt warily with the separatist tendencies of Quebec; and conscription laws were not passed in two world wars, in order not to offend the people of Quebec, though Britain and France were allies in both wars. Recently, French separatism has been more active than usual, and the language problem is definitely a threat, if not to the unity of the nation, then at least to its internal harmony.

The famous American "melting pot," which "Americanized" millions of European immigrants of all races and languages in the nineteenth century, is assumed by some American patriots to refute the idea that differences of language and race are a threat to national unity. But since language is more malleable than race, and since ethnic minorities were not localized but scattered over a broad continental expanse, it was a simple process to absorb the various languages in the dominant English language, with a compulsory public school as the chief agent of "Americanization." Intermarriage also provided some of the force of the melting pot.

But even in a nation favored with wide open spaces, an undeveloped continent rich in natural resources, and a developing industry ready to absorb a variety of peoples, the strains due to diversity of language and race on the community revealed themselves in the anti-immigrant riots of the nineteenth century and in restrictive immigration laws favoring people of North European stock and excluding Asians.

The hazards inherent in racial differentiation were of course particularly apparent in the refusal of the nation to give the Negro a decent position in the national community. From slavery days until the current racial tensions, the plight of the Negro citizen has revealed the hazard of a minority diverging too obviously and vividly from the dominant type. Thus "nature" and "organic" forces of cohesion and division reveal themselves even in a nation so favored by geography and history as to be tempted to regard community-building as purely in the domain of man's reason and conscious will. The comparative ease with which the major problem of ethnic diversity was solved may indeed have been one of the many causes of the American tendency to sing incantations to "freedom" without measuring the problems which societies face in making freedom compatible with community.

2. *The Problem of Religio-cultural Diversity*

A common religious belief may be as strong a force of cohesion in the national community, and diversity in religion may be as divisive a force as are common and diverse ethnic kinship and language. Religion is not strictly in the realm of nature, but as a unifying and dividing force not immediately under the control of human reason and conscious will, it must be placed in the category of "organism" rather than "artifact" or conscious contrivance.

Free institutions permit and encourage a diversity of religious loyalty, since it is not possible to suppress any belief for the sake of building uniformity upon the basis of a dominant religious group. But this means that free societies in Europe were forced to overcome the hazards of religious pluralism. Modern non-European communities confront even greater pluralism than did the European nations after the Renaissance and Reformation shattered the religious unity and uniformity of Europe.

The Huguenot wars in France postponed the rise of free government for a century, for the shattered religious unity of the nation prompted even such high-minded humanists as Jean Bodin to embrace monarchic absolutism in a vain effort to unify the nation.

The long evolution from religious uniformity and political absolutism to pluralism and toleration in Great Britain is a vivid reminder of the hazards of religious diversity which European nations faced and which helped to contribute to the rise of free government. Tudor nationalism and monarchic absolutism under Henry VIII seemed to solve the problem in enforcing a new uniformity under a quasi-Catholic national church. Two further attempts at uniformity, one under Queen Mary, the Catholic heir of Henry, the other under the Protestant heir, King Edward VI, were both equally repressive of competitive versions of the Christian faith before Queen Elizabeth created an Anglican synthesis between the old and the new faiths.

Yet even the Elizabethan settlement was not stable. When James succeeded Elizabeth, the settlement became unsettled. The Cromwellian Revolution, which broke out under James's heir, King Charles, revealed the power of the suppressed radical Puritan sects. The fact that the Stuart Kings brought theories of royal absolutism derived from Calvinist institutes with them on their voyage south of the border, while their subjects were informed by later Calvinist conceptions of "resistance to tyranny," was also a contributing cause.

The Cromwellian Revolution, with its Presbyterian parliament and its radical sectarian army, of course sowed the seeds of both religious dissent and democratic radicalism in the whole nation. While the Restoration under Charles II brought back the Anglican establishment, England suffered from religious tensions and dissensions for decades before it could arrive at a workable solution of its growing religious pluralism. Parliamentary authority was exercised and strengthened twice for the sake of preventing the establishment of the Catholic religion, once in an act which brought William and Mary to the throne in the "glorious revolution" of 1688, and the second time when the house of Hanover was invested with monarchic power over the British nation. In both cases, however, the issue was settled by preserving the Anglican establishment, and toleration for both Catholics and nonconformists had to wait upon the nineteenth-century development of democratic procedures. The assertion of the authority of parliament revealed both the value of free institutions in settling the issue and the strengthening of those institutions through the confrontation of religious crises. One suspects that this unique history of dealing with the problem of religious diversity is more revealing of the British genius for gradualism than of any general lesson which might be drawn for the solution of a problem confronting many new nations today. The problem of religious diversity was more easily solved in our own country than in Europe. The very extent of the diversity prompted a toleration which European nations only slowly achieved. The original colonies, peopled by refugees from contrary forms of religious absolutism, exhibited wide diversity within each colony and between the colonies. There was no sect with pretensions to being the preferred religious group. The theocracy of New England had long since been vanquished, and even the Calvinist John Adams believed in the separation of church and state, his Calvinism having been diluted with a large dose of eighteenth-century enlightenment.

The prevailing form of Protestantism was, since Roger Williams, sectarian and radical evangelicalism. Williams, in *Bloudy Tenent of Persecution,* had long since protested against politically enforced religious uniformity; and Jonathan Edwards' "Great Awakening," sweeping down the eastern seacoast, had supported Madison and Jefferson in disestablishing the Anglican church in Virginia, and in laying down the principle of the separation of church and state which was to solve the problem of religious diversity for the new nation. This diversity was to become greater in the nineteenth century, when the nation absorbed large masses of Southern European, Latin, and Slavic immigrants either of Catholic or Jewish religious heritage.

Moreover, the minorities were not strongly localized, being dispersed over the whole continent; and the coincidence of a particular religion and language was soon overcome in the melting pot on which the burgeoning nation prided itself. It did not melt down the ethnic and religious groups to a common amalgam, but the ethnic minorities soon acquired a common English tongue which prevented the reinforcement of religious by linguistic differentiation. The anti-Irish riots, the Know Nothing movement, and the rise of a nascent anti-Semitism were indications, however, of the stubbornness of these problems of heterogeneity even in a nation which took diversity in language, race, and religion for granted.

Thus, the very ease with which the problem of religious diversity was solved, because alternative solutions were impracticable or literally impossible, may have been one of the reasons which tempted the hegemonous nation of the democratic bloc to regard democratic self-government as a simple alternative or option for non-European nations, many of which face this problem in far more serious proportions than we. Our own history has prevented us from gauging the difficulties of nations with divergent religious traditions. India, for instance, possesses the two religious traditions of Hinduism and Islam, which made it impossible for the newly emancipated nation to preserve the unity it had under the British regime, while Nigeria has unsuccessfully tried to combine a politically integrated Islamic northern region and a Christian and animistic south.

Democratic self-government is a highly contrived form of community which must depend upon organic and uncontrived forms of community for its foundations. It cannot afford too many rifts in the organic forms of community established by a common language or race, or too localized and serious divisions within the community as a result of divergent religious loyalties.

Few nations have the good fortune of the United States, which harbored a multiplicity of religious groups, none of them large or dominant enough to seek uniformity through its own establishment. Toleration under the pressure of sheer necessity was rare in European history.

Lacking this favorable circumstance, either religious toleration must wait on the development of a religious faith which is vital and profound enough to distinguish between loyalty to the ultimate religious commitment and those relative and contingent values and loyalties which are compounded with devotion to God in conventional religion, or it must wait for the waning of religious loyalty under the corrosive effects of modern secularism. Religious loyalties can be very divisive, precisely because absolute claims are made in their behalf; and a pluralistic community requires an empirical consideration of relative claims from various portions of the community.

The degree of "social tissue" which binds the community together outside the realm of religious loyalty is important in overcoming religious division. All contacts in common realms of culture, the arts, and economic and social endeavor which create "social tissue" below, above, and outside the realm of religious loyalty help to undermine the force of religious division.

The European experience with religious diversity is important, for it reveals the stubbornness of the problem. But it scarcely suggests the scope in which modern non-European nations encounter the problem. They must deal not only with three religious traditions with a common Biblical root, but with a multiplicity both of high and of primitive religions.

Recent rebellions and separatist movements in African nations, such as in the originally promising Nigeria and the less promising Congo, illustrate the obstacles to the creation of integral community and democracy in primitive cultures. The triumph of nationhood and democracy over the divisive factors of language, tribal loyalties, and a multiplicity of religions will probably require a century of development. The African problems, and similar problems in Asia, to be examined in the second half of this volume, must prompt a revision of the popularly accepted utopian version of democracy, by which the triumph of this difficult but necessary instrument of community and justice is regarded as a live option for all nations in all cultures and climes.

3

THE IMPACT OF
INDUSTRIALIZATION

THE ANALYSIS OF THE PROBLEMS of diversity in race, language, and religion encountered by the national communities of Europe has revealed that nations are communities not so much of discrete individuals as of racial and cultural groups which must learn to live in harmony with each other if the nation is not to be subjected to coerced unity and uniformity. We have observed that these differences pose a particularly difficult problem for democratic societies, whether in Europe or the other continents.

However, the problems of diversity in race, language, and religion encountered in Europe, either before the birth of free governments or in the process of birth, were not as important as the problems of class and economic advantage, which were aggravated in European culture by the rise of modern industry, roughly a century after the rise of democracy.

All traditional communities had class distinctions, but the dominant class of landed wealth had both the political and economic power to enforce a common rule favorable to it, which put all other classes at a disadvantage. This dominance was not challenged seriously until the dawn of modern society. The history of empires and nations was a "history of class struggles," as the Marxist view would have it, only occasionally, when desperation prompted the peasants and the workers of the Roman and the medieval empires to futile revolt.

Modern free governments entered into history in the seventeenth and eighteenth centuries only after the classes of commerce and the craftsmen became able, by new forms of economic and social power, to challenge landed wealth. One of their instruments was the establishment and extension of the franchise. Thus free governments, to use the Lockean definition, derived their authority from the consent of the governed.

Free governments actually required centuries to extend the right of consent to all the governed. The removal of the property restriction on the right of franchise meant that the principle of consent was more than a bourgeois device, used first in the class struggle with landed wealth and denied subsequently to the workers, who were both erstwhile partners of the bourgeoisie in building a free society and its ultimate competitors in stabilizing and extending it.

Meanwhile the Industrial Revolution, with the invention of the steam engine, and the harnessing of coal and iron, was to create a seemingly catastrophic shift in power relations between the two dynamic classes of democracy. The craftsman lost both his tool and his skill to the machine. This left the worker powerless in the industrial sphere, adding economic weakness to his lack of political power.

G. D. H. Cole accurately describes this radical shift in power in early English industrialism when he writes: "The handloom weavers . . . fought a long losing battle with power-driven machinery. . . . Employers, facing acute competition and eager to make high profits . . . resisted ferociously every attempt of the workers to organize for the improvement of their conditions."[1]

The social distresses, consequent upon this radical shift in power relations in all West European industrial nations, were in fact so obvious that free societies were confronted with a most serious challenge, which they met by the tardy and tortuous process of adjusting their political and economic institutions to the new situation. Their tardiness in doing so gave the Marxist rebellion against bourgeois civilization a plausibility which, though only momentary, provided the stuff for its apocalypse of doom and utopia.

On the other hand, the modern solemn incantations to "freedom," as if that were a panacea for all social ills, have obscured the significance of what has been achieved. For free institutions have triumphed to some degree over the class biases both of the middle and the aristocratic classes. Also, there has been created by slow degrees both a public ethos concerned with the welfare of all people, and a certain equilibrium of social and political power.

This entire political and social history has made the Marxist apocalypse and derived dogma otiose in the Western world. It also has revealed that free institutions have a virtue which transcends the ideological biases both of the original progenitors of democracy and of those agents of history who are involved in the gradual adjustments of rights to rights and interest to interest. The operation of free institutions in a free society produces a common sense of justice, which is superior to that of the classes involved in the free accommodation of interests.

This sense of justice, however, does not guarantee disinter-

---

[1] G. D. H. Cole, *Introduction to Economic History, 1750–1950* (London: Macmillan, 1952), pp. 59–60.

estedness in any struggle in which a free nation is engaged with other nations. The idea of the founding fathers that imperialism and aggression were the vices of a traditional government but not of a democracy was as illusory as the subsequent Marxist idea that all political vices were the consequence of capitalism. But the history of the West does prove that a free accommodation of interests makes for a communal cohesion in which order and justice are so intimately related that the community is free of the twin evils of man's political life, despotism on the one hand and anarchy on the other.

But these triumphs of a free society must not obscure the social and political conditions which precipitated the Marxist rebellion. The rapid industrialization of feudal and primitive cultures creates conditions in the non-European world similar to those of early European industrialism. The seeming plausibility of Communism in the non-European world and its irrelevance to healthy European democracies cannot be understood without noting that Marx was wrong only in fashioning a scheme of world salvation from highly contingent historical circumstances. He was at least partly right in describing those conditions, though his polemical animus offered a caricature of the political scene.

Marx's concept of the "alienation of the worker from his humanity" was the consequence of the reduction of labor to the status of a commodity, when early industrialism gave the powerless and rightless worker no possibility of asserting his human rights in the community. Marx viewed the bourgeoisie as the devils who had invented the final evil of history and robbed the worker of all human relations. The indictment against the bourgeoisie in the *Communist Manifesto* is specific and devastating. It declares:

> The bourgeoisie, wherever it has got the upper hand, has put an end to all feudal, patriarchal, idyllic relations. It has pitilessly torn asunder the motley feudal ties that bound man to his "natural superiors," and has left remaining no other bond between man and man than naked self-interest, than callous "cash payment." It has

drowned the most heavenly ecstasies of religious fervor, of chivalrous enthusiasm, of philistine sentimentalism, in the icy waters of egotistical calculation.

Marx's view of the dictatorship of the bourgeoisie for which he desired to substitute a vaguely conceived dictatorship of the proletariat was taken from the highly contingent circumstances of French history. The period which gave him the material for his apocalypse was the fall of the Orleans Monarchy and the organization of the Second Republic in the revolution of 1848. The Republic had reinstituted universal suffrage, and indeed a contributing cause of the fall of the Orleans Monarchy was the latter's hesitancy in restoring the universal franchise, restricted by the various ventures of the Directory, the Bourbon Restoration, and the July Monarchy.

But even the most objective historians point to the fraudulent character of the democracy of the Second Republic, soon to be transmuted into the second Napoleonic Empire. Gordon Wright describes the policies of the early republic, which gave Marx so much material for his polemical use, in this way:

> By a series of hypocritical intrigues, the bourgeois politicians consciously provoked the workers' revolt in June, 1848, in order to provide an excuse for drowning the "reds" in their own blood. The Marxist and neo-Marxist thesis suggests that the bourgeois leaders were not merely narrow-minded and selfish, but wicked as well. . . . The Marxist version . . . is an attractive one, for it ties the period into a neat bundle with no loose ends. Some aspects of it, moreover, are undoubtedly sound. Many members of the bourgeoisie were openly or hypocritically bigoted and subject to panic. . . . Yet as a total explanation the thesis is more plausible than convincing. It is far too simple and systematized to fit a highly complex episode.[2]

The persistent fault of the Marxist dogma about history is that it gives a too simple and systematized version of the endlessly complex and variegated drama of history, including democratic

2 Gordon Wright, *France in Modern Times: 1760 to the Present* (Chicago: Rand McNally, 1960), pp. 169–70.

history. In this case the evidence is taken from French history, with its vain efforts to reach a viable democratic equilibrium. The birth of the Second Republic of France occurred sixteen years after the great Reform Act of 1832 in Britain. That legislative act was one chapter in the slow accommodation of a free society to the problems of modern freedom and industrialism. This development was too complex to fit the Marxist dogma. We must study the history of Europe in detail in order to separate the recurring patterns, forces, and factors which the new nations must also meet from the factors which are contingent to European history.

The new nations of Asia and Africa will confront contingent factors which make some of European history irrelevant to their purposes, but they will also meet some recurrent patterns and forces. Therefore, the prospects of the survival of free institutions in the non-European world may be partly gauged by discerning these recurrent factors and patterns in European history.

Four classes are involved in both the rise of free governments and in their adjustment to an industrial civilization. The first is the class of landed wealth, deeply involved in the traditional order, inimical to a democratic government, but capable of gradually adjusting itself to free institutions if it is not liquidated by revolutionary action, as it was in France. The history of democracy in Western Europe, as distinguished from the more consistently bourgeois cultures of the United States and the British Commonwealth nations, reveals that this class can make creative contributions to the radical adjustment from the organic collectivism of feudalism to the technical collectivism of modern industrial civilization. The British example of the gradual adjustment of landed wealth to democracy and industrialism is more vivid or better known, but the smaller nations of Western Europe, chiefly the Scandinavian nations, Belgium, and Holland, are equally good examples.

The second, and the most dynamic, class in the development both of democracy and of modern industry is that of the com-

mercial and industrial owners. They are the consistent indi-
vidualists in the drama, informed by a religiously derived sense
of individual responsibility and initiative, and molded by the
possession of more mobile and flexible forms of private property
than were the feudalists. Also, they were anxious to free their
economic activity from every political restraint, whether the
restrictive mercantilist politics of landed wealth, or the later
welfare measures of democratic states. The bourgeoisie was, of
course, not one class but a congeries of middle classes, representing commercial, banking, and industrial wealth, and frequently
the professions. In the last instance, the sense of individual
security through talent was frequently the nexus between the
professions and the businessman's sense of security won through
his own initiative.

The third class comprised the workers—originally the craftsmen, the early partners of the business classes in the creation of
free societies, and subsequently the industrial workers, for whom
the transfer of tool and talent to the power machine had the
previously described catastrophic effects. This dynamic class became, in consequence of industrialization, the chief competitors
of their erstwhile partners in the adjustment of free institutions
to modern industry.

The fourth class comprises the men of the soil, the peasants of
traditional cultures and the free yeomen and farmers of modern
culture. In the early period of democracy, their lack of literacy
made them the servants of aristocratic conservatism, as they
proved to be in the First and Second French Republics. The men
of the soil were in any case "Janus-faced," because their love of
the soil made them conservative, and sometimes excessively patriotic, while their poverty related them periodically to radical
movements, as in the nineteenth-century American populist
movement and in the innumerable peasant leagues of Europe,
before and after the rise of free government. The men of the soil
are, in any case, not as dynamic a force in modern history as
industrial owners and industrial workers. In recent years their

political power has been expressed chiefly in safeguarding their living standards in an industrial society.

In America the men of the soil have been the allies of industrial wealth since the Civil War. The Homestead Act of a Republican administration and the natural individualism of the farmer established a partnership in the Republican Party which has only eroded slightly in recent years. The American populist movement of the late nineteenth century revealed the radical propensities of the debt-ridden poor farmers. It did not alter the partnership between the farmers and the industrialists, which persisted well into the twentieth century.

If we dismiss the men of the soil as having only negative and periodic significance in the history of the adjustment of Western democracy to modern industrialism, we must center our attention on the three remaining classes and follow the shifts in their complex power relationships consequent to the rise of democracy on the one hand and the rise of industrialism on the other. But the political arena, though always concerned with power, is never a mere power struggle. Another factor is always operative. To define this factor as the moral sense of the community might assign conscience, collectively expressed, a too important position in the political order. It would be better to speak of the "ethos" of the community, and to understand that factors of morale and morality are comprehended in this ethos. One significant factor of morale, rather than morals, is the communal cohesiveness in the nation, expressed in both the implicit consent which the community gives to the authority of government, and the frequently corresponding patriotic sense of loyalty to the national community as such.

It was the defect of this morale factor in the history of France which prevented France from digesting first the bourgeois and then the industrial revolutions. The instability of regimes in the history of modern France was both the cause and the consequence of a defect in the political ethos of the nation. The rapid alternations of regimes—the First Republic, the Directory, the

Consulate, the Empire, the Bourbon Restoration, the Orleans Monarchy, the Second Republic and the second Bonapartist Empire of Louis Napoleon—did not give any regime a sufficient sense of legitimacy to speak to, and for, the nation.

The aristocratic class, though eliminated in theory by the original revolution, constantly interfered with the process of slow accommodation of the nation to new situations, after the émigrés, strengthened by the fancied injustices of the new order, returned with their ideologies sharpened by years of exile and their yearning to restore the old. Moreover, the whole assortment of empires and monarchies—Bonapartist, Bourbon, and Orleanist—left new aristocratic groups behind them. The instability of governments was thus a cause of the inability of the nation to adjust to the emerging political and economic factors of the eighteenth and nineteenth centuries. But it was also the consequence of an unresolved ideological conflict, first between the aristocracy and the bourgeoisie, and then between the latter and the emerging industrial workers.

The fact that not only Britain, but all the smaller democratic nations of Western Europe which have successfully negotiated both the democratic and the industrial revolutions are constitutional monarchies may not be an indication of the virtues of the monarchical institutions as such. But it does reveal that morale factors are most easily transmuted if the history of a nation is not subject to violent revolutionary eruptions. The symbol of the monarchy in Western Europe is the symbol of an evolutionary history in which loyalty to the nation and implicit consent for the policies of a "legitimate" government enclosed all the political frictions and competitions, and robbed the ideological struggle of its sharpness and consistency. The history of France with its failure to digest either democracy or industrialism is evidence of the importance of the morale factor in the ethos of a nation.

If we thus eliminate France in our consideration of the course of democratic adjustments to modern industry, we must turn to a comparison of Britain and the United States in order to analyze how a free society comes to terms with a shifting internal balance of power and how the ethos of a nation may influence, and be influenced by changing power relationships.

An analysis of two free societies, the British and the American, in the process of their accommodation to modern industrialism, must illumine the similar and different ways in which these two nations, the one with a feudal tradition and the other developing as a bourgeois community without a feudal background, have managed two forms of power equilibrium—political and economic—in the two great revolutions of the modern period. The first gave rise to democracy and the second adjusted free institutions to the power realities of modern industry.

1. *Political Power and the Right of Suffrage*

Political power in a free society, in which all authority is derived from the consent of the governed, naturally is inherent in the right of the citizen to give his consent—i.e., his right to exercise his franchise and vote. The voter chooses his representatives and "rulers," holds a veto power over their policies, and ultimately, though not immediately, determines the policy of the political state. This political policy is more dominant than any economic force, though both classical economics and modern Marxism have propounded the theory of the supremacy of economics over politics.

In so far as the right to vote is universal, or, more exactly, tends to become universal, in the history of free societies (even if these begin with property restrictions on the franchise), political power is an equalizing factor in democracies that tends to mitigate the inequalities in the social and economic sphere. Universal suffrage contributed to the rise of the modern welfare state, for the power of the vote exercised by the poor as well as the rich was bound to result in using the taxing power of the state to establish minimal securities for the poor and generally to lessen the economic inequalities which have always existed but which were accentuated in modern industrial civilization.

In England, where representative government had its roots in the Middle Ages, where Parliament consisted of two houses, the Lords and the Commons, the right to vote was initially only a middle-class privilege since the franchise was limited by property restrictions. It was, in any case, merely an extension of the franchise which the middle classes enjoyed in their guilds and in their city charters. Since the right was deeply rooted in English history, it was generally acknowledged as a "civil right," one of the many "rights of Englishmen." The fact that the beginnings of social justice in England predated the extension of universal suffrage demonstrates that the ethos of the community is operative in the application of principles of social justice even before the actual exercise of political power by those who feel themselves misused in the community.

The first definition of the right of suffrage as a "natural right" was propounded in the Putney debates, a kind of constitutional convention in Cromwell's army. There the radicals Wildman and Rainborough argued eloquently that the right to vote was a natural right, inherent in the rational character of man. Rainborough said: "Really I think that the poorest he that is in England hath a life to live as the greatest he; and therefore truly, Sir, I think it's clear that every man that is to live under a Government ought first by his own consent to put himself under that Government."

This first advocacy in England of the right of franchise as a natural right was not popular, even in Cromwell's army, certainly not in the army command. Ireton answered Rainborough: "If you make this the rule I think you must fly for refuge to an absolute natural Right, and you must deny all Civil Right."[3]

The Putney debates were adjourned by Cromwell when the various sects in the army failed to reach agreement on this and other questions. The right to vote was not acknowledged as a natural right and not made universal in the Cromwellian Protectorate. For that matter it was not accepted for several cen-

[3] Kenneth Bell, *Puritanism and Liberty* *(1603–1660)* (London: G. Bell and Sons, 1920), p. 81.

turies. The "glórious revolution" which put William and Mary on the throne failed to accept the implications of John Locke's *Second Treatise,* which celebrated both the revolution and the democratic principle that all just governments derive their authority from the consent of the governed.

Suffrage was gradually extended, but its ultimate universalization had to wait until the Act of 1885, when agricultural laborers were finally enfranchised. But all this did not prevent liberty from broadening down from precedent to precedent and a free society from growing by imperceptible stages until it had both a political and economic balance approximating social justice. If one is inclined to be pessimistic about democracy in non-European cultures, one must remember the slow growth of the instruments of justice in a free society in Western Europe. The various English Reform Acts of the nineteenth century—in 1832, 1867, and 1884–85—which eliminated "rotten boroughs" and purified and extended representative government were the consequence of social agitation, exhibiting the ethos of a culture more than expressing a new balance of power.

The difference was considerable between the American and the Western European experience in adjusting the equilibriums of power in both the political and the economic sphere, that is, in extending the franchise on the one hand and in gradually allowing the powerless individual worker collective power by the recognition of his right to organize and bargain collectively on the other. The property restrictions on the right of suffrage in the several member states of the new Union were subject to erosion much more rapidly than in Western Europe. On the other hand, the rational individualism which prompted this universalization of the right to vote also prevented the recognition of the right to organize and bargain collectively until well into the twentieth century.

Thus the adjustment of power in the political and economic spheres had a completely different chronology in a culture with a feudal background and one dominated by the individualism of the bourgeoisie. This difference will remind us that the many contingent elements in the history of Western democracy and industrialism must warn us against any effort to discern normative patterns in the Western experience which we may expect the non-European nations to follow.

In Britain, the extension of the franchise and the recognition of the right to organize were established almost simultaneously, prompted by social agitations which culminated in the reform acts. This development, so different from the American experience, revealed the difference in the ethos of the two nations. In the one, the landed aristocracy was dominant in prestige long after the commercial classes had risen to power, claimed the right to vote, and leavened the lump of feudalism. These feudal classes were conservative in yielding any power and prestige to the rising business classes, but they had an understanding for collective realities and responsibilities, a spirit of *noblesse oblige,* which distinguished them from the consistent individualism of the bourgeois classes.

The purification and extension of the franchise and the abolition of the Combination Acts of 1799–1800 were initiated by the Chartist agitations, which were influenced by the radicalism of the French Revolution, but also sobered by the tragic consequences of the ensuing Terror. The political fruit of the Chartist agitation was the great Reform Act of 1832, which purified representative government, extended the franchise, and made the House of Commons more responsive to the vote of the common man than it had been in the eighteenth century.

The Reform Act was passed by a combination of both democratic pressures and the threat of the use of royal authority. The monarch, who had dominated Parliament throughout the eras of Tudor and Stuart absolutism, and even in the Hanoverian age of the eighteenth century, was sufficiently amenable to the growing prestige of the House of Commons to persuade a reluctant House of Lords to pass the bill by threatening to create enough new peers to give the government a majority. The same device of royal authority as the servant of the Commons and the same threat of creating new peers were used in passing the Parliament Act of 1911, a step which put the capstone on the structure of political power in the interest of social justice in an industrial age.

Radical as the 1832 Reform Act was, it was painlessly inserted in the evolutionary process by which a free society progressively solved its problems. The English historian E. L. Woodward expressed both the radical and the evolutionary aspect of the Reform Act in these words: "Neither side found the result [of the Reform Act] as dramatic as it had expected. Yet the change was real and the act of 1832 was a turning-point in modern English history."[4]

The Reform Act, the product of the ethos of a free culture which had gradually extricated itself from the presuppositions of feudalism, in turn produced a radical shift in the basic political power inherent in the franchise, a power which would be used increasingly, particularly when extended in the Acts of 1867 and 1885, to mitigate the inequalities in the economic realm consequent upon industrialization. It was also used to induce an equalization of power in the economic realm by the abolition of the Combination Acts, which forbade the workers to organize and bargain collectively.

Thus by a gradual process the powerlessness and rightlessness of the workers was overcome. The Marxist prophecy of doom and revolution, which would abolish both the state and property, the former allegedly the instrument of the latter, was refuted. Trotsky succinctly expressed the Marxist pessimism about the bourgeois state and its inability to correct the situation of the workers, consequent upon the new industrial "means of production," long after the British experience had refuted the Marxist dogma when he wrote:

> Absolutely contrary to all the prophecies of Bernstein, Sombart, Tugan-Baranovsky, and others, the continued existence of the middle

---

[4] E. L. Woodward, *The Age of Reform: 1815–1870* (Oxford: Clarendon Press, 1938), p. 83.

classes has not softened but has rendered to the last degree more acute, the revolutionary crisis of bourgeois society. . . . The great forces of production—the shock factor in historical development— were choked in those obsolete institutions of the superstructure (private and the national state) property in which they found themselves locked by all preceding developments. . . . All these factors lead to an elemental revolt of the forces of production.[5]

Trotsky's exposition of the necessity of a violent revolution was of course prompted by the collapse of a feudal agrarian society living under monarchical absolutism. It has little to do with the history of a free society. It was typical of the restrictive dogma of Communism that it did not concern itself with the historic evidence that free institutions could gradually become emancipated from the biases of the classes which originally dominated them. British history, which instructed the Marxist revisionist Bernstein, was a vivid example of the evolutionary process.

If we turn now to the American history of the extension of the franchise as one of the elements of justice in an industrial democratic society, we find that the story is comparatively brief. Being more purely Lockean than the British, our founding fathers regarded the right to vote as a natural right, leaving historical developments to remove property distinctions in the several states. This history was so painless that it might well have prompted the usual American assumption that the young nation was the only pure democracy, or indeed the only democracy, ignoring the slow growth of democratic institutions in Western Europe under the aegis of the institution of monarchy which was being slowly transmuted to become itself a symbol and instrument of free institutions.

But any temptation to idealize American democracy will be moderated if we fully analyze the consistently bourgeois ethos of the nation, including the fact that the same individualistic presuppositions which prompted the recognition of the right to

[5] Leon Trotsky, *Terrorism and Communism: A Reply to Karl Kautsky* (Ann Arbor: University of Michigan Press, 1958) , pp. 33, 17.

vote as a natural right also postponed the recognition of the
workers' right to organize and bargain collectively as our Supreme Court persistently enjoined industrial strikes as "conspiracies in restraint of trade," thus reading the dogma of laissez
faire into the Constitution.

2. *Industrialism and Bourgeois Individualism*

Before tracing the slow acquisition of collective economic
power in the recognition of the individual worker's right to
organize and bargain collectively, we must give our attention to
the ethos of the community which beyond specific laws and institutions has always been the arbiter of justice. Since this ethos was
more consistently bourgeois in America than in the semifeudal
culture of Britain, it was oblivious to, or afraid of, all collective
interests and forces. While Thomas Jefferson was the most consistent Lockean of our founding fathers, the fear of collective or
class interests is most vividly expressed in James Madison's fear of
"faction." Madison's fear was all the more remarkable because
his realistic interpretation of the relation between "reason and
self-love" persuaded him that factions in a free society were inevitable. "By a faction," he wrote, "I understand any number of
citizens, whether amounting to a majority or a minority of the
whole, who are united and actuated by some common impulse,
passion, or interest, adverse to the rights of other citizens, or to
the permanent and aggregate interests of the community," thus
accurately defining at least one aspect of the political parties that
have, without constitutional warrant, become servants of our
political process.

Madison accurately defined the root of these "factions": "As
long as the reason of man continues fallible, and he is at liberty
to exercise it, different opinions will be formed. As long as the
connection subsists between his reason and his self-love, his
opinions and his passions will have a reciprocal influence on each
other; and the former will be objects to which the latter will

attach themselves." The primary cause of faction, according to
Madison, lay in the varying degrees of talent and the corresponding varying economic interests in the community, giving a very
realistic pre-Marxist account of the political process. But while
factions were dangerous, Madison saw clearly that the suppression of faction would lead to the totalitarian state. "There are
two methods of curing the mischiefs of faction," he wrote. "The
one, by removing its causes; the other, by controlling its effects.
There are again two methods of removing the causes of faction:
the one, by destroying the liberty which is essential to its existence; the other, by giving to every citizen the same opinions, the
same passions, and the same interests. It could never be more
truly said, than of the first remedy, that it is worse than the
disease. . . . The second expedient is as impractical as the first
would be unwise."[6]

None of the founding fathers saw more clearly that free
governments would inevitably deal with collective rather than
with purely individual interests, though this insight was expressed in the framework of an individualistic fear of faction.

Madison's insights were, in any case, not powerful enough to
leaven the lump of bourgeois individualism, which was supported by many streams of thought, including a curious later
combination of Calvinism and Spencer's "social Darwinism."
Calvinism gave a purely individual and moralistic account of the
difference between poverty and wealth, regarding them as the
punishments and rewards of vice and virtue. Spencer's "laws of
nature" were equated with "laws of God," and thus religion and
irreligion made common cause in seeking to prevent any class
from becoming an agent in the historical process by grasping
collective power to compensate for individual weakness.

Thus a nation which had negotiated the democratic revolution
successfully was even more tardy in coming to terms with the
collective realities of the industrial revolution than the nations

[6] All James Madison quotations are from *The Federalist,* No. X.

of Western Europe. Yet these nations were not exactly anxious to yield the worker collective power. To this history we must now turn.

3. *The Recognition of the Right of Collective Bargaining*

In Britain, practically the whole of the nineteenth century was occupied in slowly yielding to the pressure of the workers for three demands. One was for the extension and purification of the franchise, in other words the acquisition of political power. The second was for the intervention of the state to regulate hours and wages, job security, insurance against accidents, etc. Thus slowly the nine-hour day and the eight-hour day were established by law. At first women and children and then all workers were protected against undue hazards. Finally the taxing power was used to give the workers minimal security. In short, the workers drew on both the ethos of the nation and their own growing political power to induce political intervention in the industrial process for the sake of justice.

The third class of demands called for the abolition of the Combination Acts of 1799 and 1800, which barred workers from organizing and bargaining collectively, and prohibited industrial strikes, which were regarded as a criminal offense, even as our Supreme Court regarded them. The date of the Combination Acts properly makes the nineteenth century the arena for the emancipation of the "wage slave." It may have furnished Karl Marx, studying in the British Museum, with added evidence for his thesis of the "dictatorship of the bourgeoisie." The Chartist agitation of the 1820's and 1830's not only resulted in the Reform Act but also in one of the several abolitions of the Combination Acts which took place during the century.

The slow process of adjustment through the whole century, the victories and defeats, gradually yielded positive results which weaned the workers from the utopian schemes of the 1830's to the pragmatic and piecemeal strategies at the end of the century.

Since despair makes for absolute demands and hope persuades a hitherto defrauded segment of the population to engage in piecemeal progress, the difference marks the triumph of a free society over industrial injustice.

The Webbs characterize the difference in mood in the early and late century thus:

> But however strongly the outward features of the wave of 1889–90 may remind the student of those of 1833–4, the characteristics of the new movement significantly measure the extent of the advance, both in social theory and social methods, made by the wage-earners in the two intervening generations. Time and experience alone will show how far the empirical Socialism of the Trade Unionists of 1899, with its eclectic opportunism, its preference for municipal collectivism, its cautious adaptation of existing social structure, and its modest aspirations to a gradually increasing participation of the workmen in control, may safely be pronounced superior in practicability to the revolutionary and universal Communism of Robert Owen. In truth, the radical distinction between 1833–4 and 1889–90 is not a matter of the particular theories which inspired the outbursts. . . . "The . . . Old Trade Unionists" had placed the legislative power and civil administration of the country in the hands of a popularly elected hierarchy of representative bodies. The great engine of taxation was, for instance, under the control of the wage-earning voters instead of the land-owning class. The Home Secretary and the factory inspector, the relieving-officer and the borough surveyor, could be employed to carry out the behests of the workers instead of those of the capitalists. And thus it came about that the methods advocated by the New Unionist of 1889–94 resemble, not those of the Owenites of 1833–4, but much more the practical arts of political warfare so successfully pursued by the Junta of 1867–75.[7]

In short, a social revolution had changed a free society and had in turn been changed by it, so that it was a creative force in the practical and inevitably slow adjustment of interests which characterize democratic life. The analysis of this development by the Webbs, who believed in the "inevitability of gradualness," is not

[7] Sidney and Beatrice Webb, *The History of Trade Unionism* (rev. ed., extended to 1920; London: Longmans, Green, 1920) , pp. 417–19.

refuted by the fact that in the next decade they were so intrigued by the Russian Revolution that they wrote a rather uncritical account of the Soviet system.

It is obvious, of course, that the process of absorbing and accommodating free institutions to the Industrial Revolution was tortuous and slow. Both the ethos of the nations and the consequent change in the equilibriums of power moved by slow degrees. In politics we never deal with disembodied reason but with interested and biased participants whose preconceptions are only slowly eroded and whose instruments of power are also subject to slow change (except, of course, for the radical and catastrophic shift in power relations introduced by the power machine in the early Industrial Revolution).

The slowness of the democratic triumph over industrial problems admittedly gave Marxism its original plausibility. The question naturally arises whether many of the non-European nations may not be exposed to similar difficulties and lack the relevant political competence to insure a like triumph over industrial injustices.

But an analysis of the encounter of Western European democracy with industrialism would be incomplete without a return to the comparison between the course of history in Western Europe and the United States. The most remarkable fact in that comparison is the greater tardiness of America, both in using political power to cure social ills and in granting labor a more adequate equilibrium of power in the economic realm by recognizing the right to organize and bargain collectively. America lagged behind Europe by roughly a half century. Not until the world depression in the fourth decade of the new century was Roosevelt's New Deal able to establish the foundations of the welfare state and recognize the legal right of labor to bargain collectively.

The fact that this tardiness occurred in a nation in which the right to vote was universalized early in its history suggests that the ethos of a free society may be more influential than the actual power relations in the political and economic sphere. The ethos of our nation was, as we have noted, consistently bourgeois and individualistic, and therefore reluctant to come to terms with the collective realities and necessities of modern industrialism. The individualism of the nation may have been accentuated by the social mobility and consequent absence of class animus which was derived from the expanding economy and the advancing frontier. Some of the tardiness may also have been due to the preoccupation with the slavery issue, the Civil War, and Reconstruction, as well as to the fact that modern industrialism itself was thus retarded until the 1870's. All the social ferment and agitation by the poor farmers and workers, the result of the plutocratic dominance in the culture, was thus expressed in the last decades of the old century. The Knights of Labor were organized in 1873, and the populist movement, significantly comprising both farmers and workers, was formed in 1892.

But these historical contingencies were not as significant as the dominant individualism of a bourgeois culture, particularly in a nation in which everyone considered himself a member of the middle class, at least potentially.

Justice Louis Brandeis, whom President Wilson appointed to the Supreme Court in defiance of American conservative opinion, accurately defined the relation of American individualism to our tardiness in adjusting ourselves to the industrial revolution. Speaking to the Chicago Bar Association in 1915, Brandeis said:

Since the adoption of the federal constitution, and notably within the last fifty years, we have passed through an economic and social revolution which affected the lives of people more fundamentally than any political revolution known to history. Widespread substitution of machinery for hand labor . . . wrought changes in the condition of life which are in many respects greater than those which had occurred in civilized countries during thousands of years preceding. . . . Yet, while invention and discovery created the possibility of releasing men and women from the thraldom of drudgery, there actually came, with the introduction of the factory system and the development of the business corporation, new dangers to liberty. . . .

Political as well as economic and social science noted these revolutionary changes. But legal science—the unwritten judge-made laws as distinguished from legislation—was largely deaf and blind to them. . . . Where statutes giving expression to the new social spirit were clearly constitutional, judges, imbued with the relentless spirit of individualism often construed them away. . . . The law everywhere has a tendency to lag behind the facts of life. But in America the strain became dangerous, because constitutional limitations were invoked to stop the natural vent of legislation.[8]

Thus the social ferment of the late nineteenth century, expressed in various political and social movements, was frustrated by judicial authority, sanctifying the "relentless individualism" of the culture. Strikes were rigorously enjoined by the courts as "conspiracies in restraint of trade" and ruthlessly suppressed by federal troops under court orders. The Pullman strike in Chicago and the Carnegie Steel Company strike in Homestead resulted in violence. It was not until the turn of the century that Theodore Roosevelt with his doctrine of the New Nationalism challenged the dominant individualism with his concept of the supremacy of the "national interest" over all private interests.

The last three decades of the nineteenth century brought forth a plethora of political and labor movements that expressed the social ferment and unrest of the farmers and workers. The Populist Party was organized in 1892. It tried to ease the burden of debt-ridden farmers chiefly by a cheap-money policy. The American Federation of Labor, supplanting the Knights of Labor, was organized by Samuel Gompers in the same decade, and for the first time disavowed the vague radicalism which united the poor workers and farmers. It contented itself with the proximate ends of the right of collective bargaining for better wages and hours. Gompers declared that cooperation between the Federation and the Populists was "unnatural," since the Populist Party comprised "employing farmers and employed farmers in the country districts and mechanics and laborers in industrial centers."

[8] Alpheus Thomas Mason, *Free Government in the Making* (2d ed.; New York: Oxford University Press, 1956), p. 693.

His chief assistant, Adolph Strasser, specifically disavowed radical and utopian objectives and emphasized proximate goals. "Our organization does not consist of idealists," he said. "We have no ultimate ends. . . . We are fighting only for immediate objects—objects that can be realized in a few years."[9]

Unfortunately, the ethos of the nation was so thoroughly individualistic that it required more than a few years to realize the "immediate objects" of the workers. Throughout the century strikes continued to be suppressed by court injunction. Labor did not emerge as a strong political force until the fourth decade of the new century, when the world depression shook the complacency of the bourgeois nation and enabled a shrewd statesman, Franklin D. Roosevelt, to bring the legal and political institutions abreast of the collective necessities of modern industrialism.

Roosevelt's New Deal also brought the whole nation abreast of the social policies of modern European social democracies. In 1935, the Wagner Act for the first time legally recognized and protected the right of the workers to organize and bargain collectively. Under the cover of this new right, the semiskilled workers of the mass-production industries belatedly formed the unions of the C.I.O., thus supplementing the old craft-union structure of the American Federation of Labor.

It may be significant in indicating the rapid advance of modern industrialism that the cherished right of collective bargaining has become a less than adequate instrument of social justice only three decades after the right was legally recognized. Modern automation has confronted management and labor with so complex a problem that the old-style collective bargaining will no longer avail.[10]

A review of the complex history of the encounter of free gov-

[9] Eric F. Goldman, *Rendezvous with Destiny: A History of Modern American Reform* (New York: Alfred A. Knopf, 1952), p. 57. This work is an excellent account of the slow accommodation of the nation to industrialism.

[10] See Paul Jacobs, *Old Before Its Time: Collective Bargaining* (Santa Barbara, Calif.: Center for the Study of Democratic Institutions, 1963).

ernments with the hazards of industrial injustice in France, Britain, and America reveals that the triumph of freedom over injustice is neither as impossible as Communism avers nor as simple as American idealists are inclined to believe. Two highly contingent favorable factors are required for its success. One is that the process be under the auspices of a government with strong enough claims to legitimacy to weather the storms of adjustment and to carry the conservative portions of the population along on the road of social progress; the other, that the ethos of the nation possess the right proportion of aristocratic and bourgeois elements for a successful process of accommodation, or, lacking this proportion, enough wealth to permit delay in its accomplishment.

We must now trace the history of the encounter in two nations which were not as fortunate in possessing these components in right proportions: Germany and Italy.

4

THE ARRESTED AND
RECLAIMED DEMOCRACIES
OF WESTERN EUROPE

Nᴏᴛ ᴀʟʟ ᴏꜰ ᴛʜᴇ ɴᴀᴛɪᴏɴꜱ of Western Europe have experienced uninterrupted progress toward democracy. Italy and Germany, the one now boasting a strong democratic regime in West Germany, the other with the largest Communist Party in the West, are a reminder to the optimists that the road to free institutions is a rough one, filled at times with insuperable hazards.

Aside from their similar Fascist experience after World War I, their defeat in World War II—and of course their belated unification as nations in the latter part of the nineteenth century—there are not many similarities between the two nations.

Their tardiness in achieving nationhood had a common reason. The delays experienced by these two nations were caused by neither race nor religion, but because both were centers of the two international or imperial systems of the medieval period: church and empire.

When these two systems disintegrated under the pressures of the Renaissance and Reformation, both nations, despite their racial and linguistic unity, were divided by petty subnational sovereignties, the city-states of Italy and the little principalities and monarchies of Germany. Their tortuous road to unification is a reminder that race and language are not the only hazards to national unity; divided loyalties toward traditional sovereignties are also obstacles.

If free nations must depend on horizontal sources of cohesion such as race and language because the vertical source of government is a product of the total community, traditional governments are so dependent on the vertical source that common language and race do not avail them as sources of unity. Traditional governments, which tend to use the principle of sovereign legitimacy as a vertical source of cohesion for the community, easily become moribund. If, as in Russia, they become the source of unity in a multinational state, they readily degenerate into despotism and if, as in Germany and Italy, they divide an ethnically united people, they obviously become the source of political chaos. In both Germany and Italy, traditional governments were the primary obstacles to unification of the nation, and after unification, they also formed the principal impediment to the adjustment of the nation to modern industrialism. For, in both, a monarchical political institution was intimately related to a feudal class which prevented the two dynamic classes of industrial civilization, the bourgeoisie and the industrial workers, particularly the latter, from performing their rightful function. Thus the reason for the belated unification was in both nations intimately related to their failure to adjust to an industrial civilization.

1. *Germany*

Modern European industrialism was already in full flower when Germany was finally unified. The process was complicated by the rivalry between the waning Habsburg power of Austria and the waxing Hohenzollern power of Prussia. Prussia of course prevailed. After the wars with Denmark, Austria, and France, the Prussian king was proclaimed emperor of Germany. His imperial crown was the prize of German victory over France in the Franco-German war, made possible by Napoleon III's ineptitude and Bismarck's unscrupulousness. It was unity by "blood and iron," promised by the shrewd Chancellor to the Prussian king, who had, understandably, turned down the invitation of the Frankfurt parliament of 1848 to become the presiding monarch of a democratically conceived national federation of German states.

The Frankfurt parliament was informed by liberal principles and a patriotic desire for German unity. It was Bismarck's policy to draw a line between patriotism and the liberalism which were expressed in Frankfurt. He could do this the more easily because the liberals of the Frankfurt parliament, inexperienced in the power realities of a state, thought that ideal constitutional principles would ultimately attain their goals. The Prussian king not only rejected their offer but sought to throttle their endeavors. Some of them fled the country.

The lack of political toughness of the Frankfurt liberals was exhibited anew in the Weimar assembly, which conceived the democratic republic after the collapse of the Hohenzollern regime at the end of World War I. This lack of toughness was a contributing factor in the defeat of democracy in Germany by the conservative forces and privileged classes, whether led by Bismarck or nominally by Hindenburg. In short, the unification of the nation was undertaken by social forces which made the democratization of the nation and its accommodation to modern industrialism impossible.

The Frankfurt parliament may have influenced Bismarck to grant universal manhood suffrage in the constitution which federated the German empire under Prussian auspices; but the system of weighted voting based on property was not abolished in Prussia, and parliament had only circumscribed authority, chiefly in controlling the purse strings. The chancellor was not responsible to it but to the emperor. The socialist leader Karl Liebknecht later called the parliament nothing more than a fig leaf for monarchical absolutism.

The eminent English historian of Germany G. Barraclough defined the unified state created by Bismarck thus: "Although Germany in 1871 secured unity, it was not a unity expressed in self-government by the German people; the new state was designed not to represent the will of the German people but to maintain, as in generations past, the subjection of the people to the will of a privileged minority."[1]

The industrial age, which in other parts of Europe introduced the new industrial owners as competitors of landed wealth, thus created in Germany under Bismarck's shrewd·manipulation a partnership, at the expense of the industrial workers, between the industrialists and an aristocracy devoted to the arts of war. The partnership gave the industrialists and bankers the economic advantages of a national realm of commerce, and later the economic opportunities of imperial expansion. Economically, the poorer aristocrats were the pensioners of the industrialists. But politically and socially, the Junkers, who controlled the army and the government bureaucracy, outranked the industrialists. No businessman was admitted to the court until World War I. The partnership which, in England, gradually became the "Whig aristocracy," with democratic leanings developed under free parliamentary institutions, produced in Germany an only slightly modified absolutist state, with tremendous industrial and military power, in which the Junkers wielded the weapons and the industrialists became their armorers. This artfully con-

[1] G. Barraclough, *The Origins of Modern Germany* (Oxford: Basil Blackwell, 1947), p. 425.

structed alliance between two classes at the expense of the workers did not outlast Russian absolutism, despite its industrial efficiency. The Hohenzollern empire was doomed by the same world war which doomed the Czarist empire.

The growing power of the industrial workers could meanwhile not be inhibited or suppressed. Trade unions were legalized in 1869, and the Social Democratic Party was organized in 1875, only four years after the birth of the empire. Bismarck sought to outlaw both in 1878 and to woo the workers with social-security legislation, anticipating British legislation by decades and that of America by a half century.

But neither suppression nor bribery was able to solve the problem. In the election of 1890, the Socialists polled 1.5 million votes and the conservative coalition behind Bismarck lost 85 of its parliamentary seats, dropping from 220 to 135. The result was catastrophic. Bismarck was defeated. The Kaiser could not risk his throne in another attempt of suppression and therefore dismissed him. Meanwhile the labor unions continued to grow, reaching a membership of 278,000 in 1891.

The partnership between a politically inept but militarily efficient aristocracy and a politically conservative and socially unrecognized group of industrial owners prevented Bismarck's successor from allaying the unrest. In the election of 1903, the Socialists polled a third of the total vote—3 million out of 9 million votes cast.

While no modern historian places the blame for World War I solely on Germany, the unresolved social contradictions of its industrial life undoubtedly made for an increasingly hazardous foreign policy. The defeat of Germany in that war, and the collapse of the Hohenzollern empire, is a matter of history. In this context it is important to note the tragic failure of the Weimar Republic after the collapse of the monarchy to solve the problems of democracy and industrialism. The collapse of the empire was a foregone conclusion. The failure of Weimar, equipped with all the latest democratic gadgets, is another and much sadder story.

The Weimar assembly, as previously noted, was lacking in political toughness as much as the Frankfurt parliament of the mid-nineteenth century. The similarity was the more remarkable because the Socialist Party was now the largest party of the republic, and Socialists, not middle-class idealists, dominated Weimar. But their socialism was shorn of its revolutionary ardor without having acquired true comprehension of the power realities of the political order. Whether they were "orthodox" Marxist determinists waiting for historical inevitabilities to bring them victory or whether they followed the "revisionism" of Eduard Bernstein, who had learned much from the British democratic experience but did not understand Germany's political backwardness, the Socialists were tame.

Barraclough describes the reason for the failure of the Socialists of Weimar succinctly:

> Thus, through the anxious, cautious constitutionalism of the Social Democrat leaders, Ebert and Scheidemann, none of the three fundamental reforms—democratization of the army, public control of heavy industry, redistribution of landed property—were secured; and the reason was that to secure them it would have been necessary to rely on extra-parliamentary means and have recourse to popular pressure. Such a policy was alien to the whole character of the Social Democratic leadership, which had for decades past known no higher aim than the attainment of parliamentary democracy and the representation in parliament of working-class interests [pp. 441–42].

The tragic failure of the Weimar Republic, which brought with it the rise of a demonic totalitarianism that made Hohenzollern absolutism seem to be the seat of virtue by comparison was of course due to many causes. The republican regime might have survived if the world depression had not aggravated the social chaos, inflation, and middle-class furies incident upon the defeat of a once-proud nation. But the chief causes were undoubtedly the failure of the new democracy to deal radically with the social forces and powers of the traditional order.

Since revolutions usually deal with traditionally established powers with an excess of revolutionary fanaticism and assume that their liquidation will insure perfect justice, the anxious and cautious constitutionalism of the Weimar Republic was something of a revolutionary anomaly. It was the more remarkable for taking place in the birthplace of Marx. Surely one of the many lessons free governments can learn from this tragic failure is that reliance on "constitutional" authority is illusory. Constitutions have authority only to the degree that they embody the ethos of a community and express its traditional loyalties or a new balance of social forces.

A new constitution that does not eliminate or challenge old social forces and loyalties and that fails to give political recognition to the new forces behind it is bound to lack authority. For the authority lies not so much in the written document as in the social climate and the equilibrium of social forces that create the constitution. The Weimar constitution existed in a social vacuum. The military and the industrial powers remained unchallenged and uncurbed. Both these forces actively helped Hitler's demonic political movement come to power, first by "constitutional" means and ultimately by extraconstitutional seizure of power.[2]

The Nazi regime, which ruled Germany by force and fraud from 1933 to the collapse of the nation in 1945, is not part of the history of free institutions, except in so far as it inadvertently razed the loyalties, institutions, and traditions of both imperial and republican Germany and thus prepared the political ground for a new democracy in the Western part of the nation. The Bonn Republic was of course organized only in the three Western zones of the vanquished nation. The Russian-occupied portion became the small puppet state of East Germany. The division has not yet been healed, and thus the history of the Bonn Republic is the history of only one part of the divided nation. Devastation and division were the tragic legacies of Hitler's Nazi regime.

[2] The help given this revolution by both the military command and the big industrialists has been accurately traced in Wheeler-Bennett's *Nemesis of Power* (2nd ed.; London: Macmillan, 1964).

While the parliamentary and other institutions of the Bonn Republic were more soberly conceived than those of the Weimar Republic, the striking success of the former compared to the failure of the latter is not primarily due to constitutional differences. Not only did the dismal wreck of Hitler's policy leave the nation sick with disillusionment about all authoritarian regimes with their repression at home and adventurism abroad, but it also leveled the social eminences in state and economy and destroyed the centers of political prestige that might challenge the future. Nazism left a *tabula rasa* upon which a free society could be built. For these and other reasons, the new *Bundesrepublik* of Bonn did not repeat the mistakes of the Weimar Republic.

The chaotic economic life of the devastated nation was partially overcome by a currency reform of 1948, which gave the new nation a hard currency. The united nation of the Western zones came into being in 1949. Since its inception, West Germany has experienced almost uninterrupted economic expansion. The refugees from the Eastern zone furnished the manpower for a growing economy, and the devastated factories of the defeated nation were replaced with highly modernized technical equipment, superior to that of other nations of Europe. At the birth of the new republic, the country elected to be governed by the Christian Democratic Union, with Chancellor Adenauer as head of the government and Economics Minister Ludwig Erhard furnishing the blueprints for a mixed economy and the outlines of a welfare state. The economy was of course aided by America's Marshall Plan, designed for the whole of devastated Western Europe.

The political life of the new regime was determined by two parties. The Social Democrats, who had once dominated democratic politics in the Weimar Republic, were diminished in strength by the creation of the Socialist Unity Party in East Germany. Only the Red Army could force this unity, designed by Russia for the whole of Western Europe. In the Bonn Republic the Social Democrats became a minority party, though still powerful. The Christian Democrats were in the majority, and their leader, Chancellor Konrad Adenauer, came to be the architect of the political life of the new Germany.

The new Christian Democratic Union was influenced by the Centrum of the Weimar Republic, a party which represented the industrial Rhineland and mirrored not only Catholic social principles but also the interests of the industrial workers organized in Catholic labor unions, thus demonstrating the capacity of the Catholic Church to keep the support of industrial workers.

Although the Christian Democrats were not a purely Catholic party, having absorbed many Protestants, the Centrum furnished the social philosophy of the new party. The former Bavarian People's Party, which expressed an agrarian conservatism unable to make common political cause with the old Centrum, was ideologically submerged in the new Christian Democratic Party and influenced its Bavarian section, the Christian Social Union. This united party managed to gain a parliamentary majority over the Social Democrats by an alliance with the Free Democrats, a small party representing business interests.

Under the pressure of the occupying powers, a united trade-union movement was formed comprising the former Catholic and Socialist unions. The mixed economy and the social-security guarantees of the modern welfare state provided for a tolerably equitable distribution of the newly gained wealth and a tolerable industrial peace in a nation whose political heritage included the "class struggle" of Karl Marx. Everything that had seemed impossible in the days of Hohenzollern rule or in the Weimar Republic now entered the realm of political possibilities.

The political philosophy of the Christian Democratic Party, which has presided over the political and economic revival of Germany, deserves special study, particularly by Western liberals who proceed from the assumption that Catholicism is hopelessly involved in feudal conservatism. Catholicism was unable to extricate itself from feudalism without the help of various modern cultural and economic forces; but once it did extricate itself, as in Western Europe, it performed a creative function in adjusting modern free governments to modern industrialism. The reason for its "liberalism" has not been fully understood. Because it has not been influenced by the individualism of classical liberalism, it has been able to transfer its conviction about the social substance of human existence from the organic collectivism of the Middle Ages to the collective requirements of industrial civilization without great difficulty.

The social teachings of modern Catholicism were first expounded in Pope Leo XIII's encyclical *Rerum Novarum,* and since elaborated by many of his successors, including the late John XXIII in his encyclical *Mater et Magistra.* The social doctrine of the popes emphasized the right of workers to organize and bargain collectively. These social teachings were *inter alia* responsible for holding the loyalty of the workers in such industrial regions as the German Ruhr. On the other hand, the Church's doctrine about the right of private property, which it defended, provided that it was subordinated to political and moral responsibilities, was acceptable to the industrial owners in a nation strongly under Socialist influence.

In the Weimar Republic, the critics of Catholic social thought believed that its efforts to transcend the "class struggle" between owners and workers constituted a source of confusion, which was compounded by the fact that religious loyalty prevented the organization of a unified trade-union movement, dividing the workers into Catholic and Socialist unions.

In the Bonn Republic the fusion of the trade unions into a single federation has eliminated some of these confusions and enabled German unionism to be a more creative force in the new Germany. Meanwhile the Social Democratic Party, after initial efforts to capitalize on a revived German nationalism, has followed a pragmatic and nondogmatic course which has gained it increasing support. In 1967, the Christian Democrats formed an alliance with the Social Democrats in which Willy Brandt be-

came Foreign Minister under the new Chancellor, Kurt Kie-
singer. There are sufficient differences in social policy and sufficient similarities between the two parties to obviate the old "class
struggle" of Germany and to insure both flexibility and continuity of government in the republic.

Thus from the debris of the Nazi regime and the devastation
of defeat in a cruel war, from the remnants of the abortive
democratic regime of Weimar, and against the background of a
long authoritarian history under monarchical absolutism, there
arose a healthy democratic government and nation which has
solved the problem of modern industrialism more adequately
than any other Continental nation. In the short span of years
since its establishment, the Bonn Republic not only has found
tolerable solutions to domestic problems, but as a member of
NATO, the Common Market, and Euratom, it has achieved
reconciliation with France and become a creative part of a
rejuvenated Western Europe, a strong bastion against Communism, more steadfast than any nation on the Continent.

The history of the Bonn Republic, with its remarkable rejuvenation of the nation, its modernization of war-devastated
industrial installations, its employment of refugees from the East
to man its expanding industry, its healthy political life on the
razed ground of old sovereignties, is one of the most remarkable
triumphs of free institutions over previous disasters.

The belated emergence of a free society in Germany reveals
some interesting facets of the truism that democracy is at once a
luxury and a necessity for justice. Democracy proved to be a
luxury that was beyond the resources of this highly talented
nation, because its belated unification made for an alliance of an
aristocracy gifted in the arts of war, and a plutocracy gifted in
industrial pursuits. But both classes were politically inexperienced. The industrial workers, without a gradual introduction
into the arts of politics, prematurely turned their revolutionary
zeal into a tame acceptance of the sovereignties and traditions of
the authoritarian order.

Two eras of domestic repression and foreign adventures that resulted in two wars and devastating defeats revealed that only a free government could secure internal justice, and though it could not guarantee international peace, it could at least prevent military adventurism. Thus a luxury turned out to be a necessity, and a gifted but war-torn nation finally reached the goal of domestic and foreign tranquility which political freedom can not guarantee but which it is disposed to achieve more certainly than any authoritarian government.

2. *Italy*

The history of the defeat of democratic institutions in Italy and their subsequent rejuvenation parallels in many respects the history of Germany. The similarities between the two nations begin with their belated and almost simultaneous unification. Italian unity was not complete until the city of Rome was taken in 1870, nine years after the first unification, when Germany's defeat of France offered a chance to snatch the Eternal City from French overlordship and papal sovereignty.

The Italian experience is significant in the context of this study for two reasons. On the one hand, Italy is an undeveloped nation which achieved a belated industrial development. Its conditions and problems are therefore more akin to those of the new nations than to those of any other West European nation. But, on the other hand, Italian history is a minor obbligato to the fierce *Götterdämmerung* of German history because the same social forces were operative there in flaccid rather than in dynamic forms. Italian feudalism was stagnant. The aristocracy, unlike the German Junkers, was not skilled in the arts of war. They were on the whole absent and uncreative landlords living luxuriously in the capital while their peasants starved.

The Italian peasants were largely illiterate, the businessmen were not enterprising, and the industrial workers, who arrived at their Marxist philosophy belatedly, compounded Marxism with syndicalism, thus making the opposite mistake of the Weimar workers: Instead of seeking gradual accommodation in a free society, they favored the revolutionary method of the general strike.

The peculiar but inevitable consequence of Italian unification, involving an industrial north and an agrarian center and south, was the existence of two cultures side by side, neither of which seriously influenced the other. The miserable conditions of the peasants in the backward agrarian regions, their poverty and illiteracy, continue to this day. Though the unified nation gave more opportunities for commercial and industrial enterprise, it had a negative effect on the backward agrarian regions, which were unable to compete with the more efficient regions.

Italy was unified by the combined efforts of three very different men: Mazzini, the poet and dreamer of Italian nationalism, who thought of Italy as a messianic nation and dreamed of a "third Rome" which would combine patriotism with the love of mankind; Garibaldi, the soldier of guerrilla warfare, whose martial spirit provided the force for the conquest of the reluctant fragments of the Italian nation; and Cavour, the statesman of Piedmont, without whose political shrewdness unification could never have been achieved.

The unification, which took place at the parliament of 1861, made the house of Savoy the center of loyalty that would presumably be the cohesive force of the diverse regions rescued from Austrian sovereignty, French overlordship, and papal dominion.

Venice was rescued from Austrian sovereignty by a war in 1866, in which Italy was allied with Prussia, but the French overlordship of Rome was not abrogated until Napoleon III was defeated by the Germans in 1870. The unification of Italy was thus a by-product of the rise of the German empire to glory and the German nation to unity. The popes did not recognize the unification of Italy until the concordat with Mussolini in 1929.

The weakness of Italy as a free government responsive to the will of all the people was obvious in the original constitution, which unified the realm under the sovereignty of a king of Piedmont, certainly not the most powerful of the Italian states. The cabinet was responsible to the king, not to parliament. The liberalism of Cavour, and the republicanism of both Mazzini and Garibaldi, gave parliamentary institutions more democratic relevance than they had in Prussia. Nevertheless, in critical situations the king and cabinet acted without parliament, notably in the decision taking Italy into World War I on the side of Britain and France, in giving Mussolini the premiership after his march on Rome, and in dismissing him after the Italian defeat in World War II.

From the beginning, the limits of the franchise indicated the limits of freedom in this constitutional monarchy. Of 22 million inhabitants of unified Italy, only 500,000 were empowered to vote and only 300,000 exercised that right.[3] The franchise was first extended in 1882 and then more widely by the act of 1911–12.[4] But the extension, which satisfied the politically radical and articulate industrial workers also gave illiterate peasants the vote. The distinguished criminologist Lombroso criticized the universal franchise for this very reason. The point at issue is important for the policies of the new democracies, many of whom are faced with the problem of illiteracy among the voters.

The government of Cavour, who died shortly after unification, and those of his successors were informed by a philosophy of bourgeois "liberalism," which meant, in effect, bourgeois conservatism. Cavour's successors "destroyed the economic barriers that had previously divided the various Italian states, thereby exposing the less efficient and backward enterprises of the center and south to the competition of the more advanced north."

The political life of the new nation was preoccupied with the difficulties of unifying the diverse elements of the various states,

---

[3] Denis Mack Smith, *Italy: A Modern History* (Ann Arbor: University of Michigan Press, 1959), pp. 31, 257.

[4] Norman Kogan, *The Government of Italy* (New York: Thomas Y. Crowell, 1962), p. 3.

so that it would be useless to look for a pattern of right and left in its history. Cavour and his successors governed as Walpole governed Britain in the first part of the eighteenth century. Governments were *ad hoc* coteries of patrons and their clients. The three founders of the nation were all, in different ways, anticlerical, but the issue of church and state was bound to be in the forefront in a predominantly Catholic nation whose prime minister had adopted the slogan "A free church in a free state." But even the issue of clericalism was not a partisan one. Many of the governments formed had both clerical and anticlerical members.

After 1876, the conservative liberals were succeeded by a leftist government whose radicalism consisted chiefly in the advocacy of compulsory education and the extension of the suffrage. Changes of government from right and left meant little in coming to terms with increased industrialism, which was, in any case, developed not by an enterprising middle class but by a government preoccupied with foreign policy and national prestige.

Norman Kogan writes:

> From 1861 to World War I, all Italian governments put railways, public works, the army, the navy, and the merchant marine ahead of education, social welfare and housing. Expenditures for the military were unusually heavy, 30 to 40 per cent of the annual budget being devoted to this purpose during these years [p. 5].

Thus modern capitalism developed under state auspices and the old liberalism was corrupted by a protectionist policy and by high-cost heavy industry designed to furnish the sinews of war. Nationalism and preoccupation with national prestige eroded the difference between Cavour's liberalism and Bismarck's illiberal nationalism and obscured the original passions of Mazzini and Garibaldi. Increased taxation added to the burdens of a poor people already suffering under excessive taxes of the unified state. Since industrial development affected the backward feudal lords and peasants very little, even this gain in the industrial parts of Italy aggravated the poverty of the agrarian regions.

Alexander Dumas described the contrast between wealth and poverty in feudal Italy in 1862 in terms that were to change little in the next fifty years:

> While the *signore* feeds his dogs on white bread, the people live on roots and grass, eked out with an insufficient quantity of coarse bread. The *signore* puts his horse in stables shut in from the winds and the rain and properly paved. His peasants live in damp, unhealthy hovels, open to all the winds, without windows, without a roof. The whole family will sleep on the same bed of straw, in the same room with their donkey, their pig, and their chickens.[5]

The agricultural poor engaged in sporadic revolts, which were usually put down mercilessly. The growing urban industrial proletariat meanwhile became organized. Though the anarchist and syndicalist doctrines of the 1880's gave way to Marxist theory, they were sufficiently influential to prompt labor to rely on the strike, preferably the general strike, rather than on collective bargaining to attain its goals. Thus the seeds were sown for a class war within the confines of a free community, but one which lacked instruments for a gradual accommodation of competing rights and interests.

The liberal administration of Giovanni Giolitti tried to meet the desires of the poor and to alleviate the causes of agrarian unrest rather than suppress their resentful riots. Railroads and public utilities were nationalized. Laws for the protection of laborers, particularly of women and children, were passed at the end of the century; and the foundations of a social-security program were laid. But Italy was too poor to institute an adequate welfare program.

Moreover, Bismarck's experience several decades earlier had shown that social welfare would not satisfy an industrial proletariat that felt itself disinherited, particularly once it becomes imbued with revolutionary doctrine. The entrance of Italy into World War I, its mounting debt and tax burden, and the disappointment with the fruits of its victory—all these brought the

[5] Denis Mack Smith, *op. cit.,* p. 232.

war of the classes to a pitch of unrest, when Mussolini, an ex-
Socialist, found that his hour had struck and seized the opportunity for his "March on Rome."

Mussolini, like Hitler, came to power "constitutionally" in the
sense that the king invited him to become prime minister,
though he did not have a parliamentary majority to support him.
Like Hitler, he soon remedied the situation by elections in which
intimidation and force produced the necessary votes. The old
liberalism nourished by Giolitti collapsed. The industrial
groups, fearing social unrest and the power of the trade unions,
connived with his seizure of power because the prohibition of
strikes gave them freedom from labor pressure. They particularly
feared the two growing "mass" parties, the Socialists, and a
Catholic party organized by Don Sturzo, which threatened to put
the social principles of *Rerum Novarum* into action, thus promising a new thrust of modern Catholicism into the politics of
Italy.

Mussolini's "corporate state," gradually elaborated as he became secure in power, was a façade. The "corporations" in theory
comprised management, unions, and the political state, but in
practice they gave the state control over the economy, with the
ministries acting as tools of the industrial interests. The Church
was neutralized through a concordat with the Vatican which
resolved the old "Roman question" and established Catholicism
as the official religion in a country for which Cavour had
dreamed a "free church in a free state."

The achievements of Fascism were hollow, and the pretensions
of Mussolini to rejuvenate Italy were to be tragically refuted in
World War II. But meanwhile Mussolini had killed democracy,
robbed the workers of the right to bargain collectively or strike,
and ruined the new Catholic party with his concordat with the
Pope. Mussolini's despotism was neither as cruel, as thorough-
going, nor as efficient as Hitler's, but the two forms of Fascism
were sufficiently alike to point up the tragic parallel between the
defeat of democracy in Germany and Italy.

In both cases the original free institutions were not sufficiently robust to assert their authority against the power of landed wealth and industrial capital, nor to establish a new equilibrium of power between management and industrial workers which would bring the individual freedoms of democracy into accord with the collective realities of modern industrialism. Mussolini, not unlike Hitler, had merely brushed off the restraints of the liberal state to give the dominant powers of the old order freedom under the guise of a new philosophy. Norman Kogan writes:

> Mussolini neutralized big business by giving it what it wanted in the way of economic rewards and security from labor troubles; he neutralized the civil bureaucracy by raising salaries, protecting it from and at the same time threatening it with the party appointees; he neutralized the Royal Armed Forces by a policy of military expansion and enlargement of the size of the armed forces while at the same time threatening them with the Fascist Militia. He neutralized the Catholic Church, first by suppressing Marxist parties and liberal anticlericalism, and then by coming to terms on a solution of the Roman question [p. 15].

Fascism, of course, collapsed with the ignominious defeat of Italy in World War II, into which it was led by Mussolini's foreign-policy adventures in cooperation with Hitler. The democracies, prematurely defined as "moribund" by both dictators, proved victorious. It was easy for the timid king to dismiss Mussolini without bloodshed after the Fascist "Grand Council" voted lack of confidence in him. The whole system collapsed with his dismissal and the defeat of Italy.

The Savoy dynasty did not survive the defeat of Fascism and the nation. The king was too deeply implicated in the Fascist horrors to render his excuse that a monarch must not be held responsible for the acts of his ministers plausible to the voters. The ambiguity in the conception of a constitutional monarchy in Italy, obvious since the days of unification, now took vengeance upon a constitutional monarch who, because he was not responsible to parliament, could not be regarded as an instrument of true democracy.

In the plebiscite of 1946, 12 million votes were cast against the monarchy and only 10 million for it. Henceforth a president would head the parliamentary democracy. The Christian Democrats, an amorphous centrist party under Catholic auspices, came to power, but in only one election did it win an absolute majority of the seats in parliament. Usually its majority was attained by coalitions either with the various right-of-center parties or with the Democratic Socialists under Sarragat on the left.

The party was lead by De Gasperi, a disciple of Don Sturzo, whose Catholic party had been suppressed by agreement between the Vatican and Mussolini. But the new and larger party was more amorphous than the Populari. It represented divergent social and political interests from right to left, and its lack of cohesiveness made for instability in its rule. The Socialist Party was divided between a reformist section, which voted with the Christian Democrats, and a maximalist section, which voted with the Communists. From the beginning of the new parliamentary regime, the Communist Party gained about 25 per cent of the vote; it became the strongest Communist Party in Western Europe.

The appeal of Communism to the Italian voters testifies to the unsolved social and economic problems in the nation. But this remarkable strength of Communism in a Catholic nation is still something of a mystery and subject to various interpretations. On the economic issue it may be significant that Communism has considerable appeal for the agricultural poor, whose lot is as difficult now as it was fifty years ago. The gifted Italian novelist Ignazio Silone, who has since forsworn his Communism, was prompted to join the Communist Party by agrarian rather than industrial inequalities. Italy, in short, still suffers from an unreconstructed feudalism.

One of the political rather than economic reasons for Communist strength is the fact that the Communist Party is a residuary legatee of the anticlericalism which has persisted in the nation since its founding, and of which Mazzini and Garibaldi are the symbols. The fact that Italy's politics is now dominated by a clerical party suspected of being a tool of the Church has given new strength to this anticlerical tradition. Furthermore, the strength of Communism can be partly explained by its policy of hiding its revolutionary character under domestic reformism, and its ability to come to the aid of the local poor within the framework of the existing system.

An analysis of the similarities and differences in the two reclaimed democracies of Germany and Italy allows some tentative conclusions about both the perils to the democratic cause in the unresolved problems of modern industrialism and the causes for a return to free government when alternative governments have proved by their domestic oppression and foreign adventures that responsible democracy, while not easy to achieve amid the hazards of modern industrial civilization, is the only safeguard against the abuses of irresponsible power.

The similarities and differences between Germany and Italy are as significant in the era of their democratic reconstruction as they were in the era in which inadequate democratic instruments propelled them toward Fascism and war. The obvious similarity is that the political life of both is guided by a Catholic-influenced party, the Christian Democrats. However, the German party has an inner consistency and cohesiveness which the Italian lacks. Furthermore it is opposed by a strong, united Social Democratic Party, while the Italian left has been divided into two Socialist Parties (reunited in October, 1966) and a large Communist Party.

The stronger consistency and cohesion of the German party is partly explained by its history of transcending and modifying the differences of owners and workers in the highly industrialized and politically sophisticated Ruhr and Rhineland regions. Furthermore it does not have to deal with the residual problems of feudalism. The domain of the former Junkers is in Eastern Germany.

But the important difference is that the German party articu-

lates modern Catholic social principles in a culturally and religiously pluralistic nation, while the Italian party functions in a
nation in which a single church is predominant and the danger
that a religious party will use religious loyalties to obscure rather
than modify economic interests and competition is enhanced.
This raises the question whether democratic health can ever be
achieved in a culture that is not genuinely pluralistic. For only
such a pluralism, the initial peril of free societies, can be the
perennial resource of their freedom. Democracies live by the
perpetual accommodation of rights, interests, and convictions in
free decisions. These forms of explicit consent must of course
have a background of implicit loyalty to the whole community
and its system of government. It is always preferable for the
strands of communal cohesion to be many rather than one, and
that they run across the strands of competition and tension which
every community encounters and which a free community can
solve with minimal coercion only when the strands of cohesion
and loyalty are so strong and complex that they do not coincide
with the specific points of conflict and tension.

The future of Italian democracy is not sealed, whether for
health or continued weakness. Our former Ambassador to Brazil,
Lincoln Gordon, depicts a brighter economic future for Italy in
comparing Italian economic conditions with those of Brazil. He
writes:

Italy too is a Latin country, small in size compared to Brazil but
with many resemblances. It has a mountainous and difficult terrain.
For generations its South has been a depressed area like Brazil's
Northeast. Italy lacks adequate fuel resources. It has a great industrial
center in Milan remarkably similar to that of its Brazilian sister city
of São Paulo. It has suffered from inflation and from long periods of
economic stagnation. It has had a desperate problem of unemployment which in the early years of the Marshall Plan seemed incurable.
Despite these obstacles, Italian industrial production has more than
doubled since 1953, increasing last year alone by 15 per cent. Gross
production has increased by 7½ per cent a year. The specter of unemployment no longer looms as a threat to social and political stabil-

ity. . . . How has this been done? By a combination of sound financial policy which gave Italy ten years of stable prices, the vigorous promotion of domestic and foreign private investment, the careful planning of public investment with special emphasis on the depressed South, the fruitful application of foreign assistance from the United States and elsewhere, the opening up of Italian enterprise to competitive stimulus through the European common market, the expansion and diversification of exports, and the modernization of management and labor skills through education, training, and the stimulation of higher productivity. In all of the cases of free world development, public investment and private investment, domestic investment and foreign investment have worked side by side. . . . Southern peasants, who used to accept ill health and miserable living conditions as the permanent lot of mankind, now are beginning to get decent housing and to find, through education, opportunities for their children which would have seemed unbelievable a generation ago.[6]

The historical facts may be duller than the bright hues of this picture, but it is undeniable that both the Marshall Plan and entry into the European Common Market have rejuvenated the economic life of Italy and may ultimately affect its political life.

The tortuous road by which these two arrested and reclaimed democracies, Germany and Italy, first lost and then rewon free governments is a vivid reminder that modern industrialism is a great hazard to community when ancient sovereignties and traditions aggravate rather than mitigate the inequalities of traditional feudalism. But if free governments have the resources to balance the social forces which must be brought into the field of free accommodation of collective interests, freedom becomes indeed the servant of justice and community.

This is the lesson which both the victories and the defeats of democracy in European culture hold for the struggle, now in global dimensions, to garner the wealth of advancing technics without allowing technical developments to aggravate the inequalities of traditional and organic societies. It is on this issue

[6] Lincoln Gordon, *A New Deal for Latin America: The Alliance for Progress* (Cambridge, Mass.: Harvard University Press, 1963), pp. 23 ff.

that one can claim confidently that the disagreement between Communism and the "West" is indeed a controversy between a dogmatic and an empirical approach to a complex problem. If the statesmanship is wise enough and the traditions and forces of the past are not too stubborn, the prospects for the growth of free government in the world are not too dim.

5

THE LESSONS OF THE
DEMOCRATIC EXPERIENCE
IN WESTERN HISTORY

OUR STUDY OF EUROPEAN DEMOCRACY has shown three constant prerequisites of free governments: (1) the unity and solidarity of the community, sufficiently strong to allow the free play of competitive interests without endangering the unity of the community itself; (2) a belief in the freedom of the individual and appreciation of his worth; and (3) a tolerable harmony and equilibrium of social and political and economic forces necessary to establish an approximation of social justice.

But in the history of Europe these constants were involved in all manner of historical contingency. It is therefore necessary to

isolate and distinguish these constants from the contingencies of
Western history in order to avoid the error of making Western
history rigidly normative for all free government in contemporary world politics.

These prerequisites do not have equal emphasis in Western
bourgeois democracy. There the first prerequisite is taken for
granted probably because the ethnic and linguistic unification of
these nations preceded the rise of free governments. The third is
a belated but necessary achievement in the West, accomplished
in the nineteenth-century encounter between democracy and
modern industrialism. The second prerequisite, the belief in
individual freedom, has been unduly emphasized in bourgeois
democracy. The unique circumstances of middle-class life may
have prompted this undue emphasis, which tended to obscure the
organic aspects of community and the social character of human
existence.

1. *Community Solidarity and Literacy*

The obvious cultural and linguistic pluralism of free communities would seem to render this prerequisite very paradoxi-
cal. It is nevertheless important to emphasize that a government
deriving its authority from the consent of the whole community
and lacking the authority of a unifying sanctified monarchy is
able to use only a limited amount of coercion for the sake of
unity and is bound to find deep ethnic or cultural rifts in the
community, hazardous to the very existence of the community.

The integral, i.e., national, communities of the West triumphed over ethnic, linguistic, and cultural diversities in many
and highly contingent ways. Most of the triumphs preceded the
rise of free governments. They are therefore not normative for
modern nations which are under the necessity of achieving both
unity and freedom in one era. On the other hand, the hazards of
religio-cultural diversity frequently prompted nations to establish freedom for the sake of national unity. The American

experience is a particularly vivid example of such a development.

The triumph over orally transmitted dialects which made national unity possible was largely the result of the invention of printing and the attainment of literacy. In view of the low standard of literacy in most of the modern nontechnical nations, the question arises whether any of the new nations have a comparable force of unity. The printed word may be exportable; but the common school which teaches the art of reading is not.

Cultural and technical forms of competence, built on the foundation of literacy, are in fact the chief instruments of all three forms of basic requisites of a free community. They support communal unity by helping one language triumph over dialects, and also by enabling various communities of interest and vocation to create a complex social tissue which is bound together by various ties which are unrelated to the political problems dividing the nation at any given moment.

The same cultural and technical forms of competence encourage individual freedom by giving the individual the ability and inclination to transcend or defy traditional organic loyalties, as well as the capacity to trust in his own ability to defend his interests. They also give different groups the capacity to state and to defend their collective interests and to organize for the attainment of their ends. This competence, therefore, contributes to the achievement of a tolerable equilibrium of social power and prevents any group from becoming dispirited, disaffected, and rebellious against the democratic process of a fluid and gradual adjustment of interests for the sake of equal justice. The role of articulate Negro students in the Negro rebellion in the United States is an interesting example of the value of intellectual competence in the achievement of an adequate equilibrium of social power.

In the light of these facts it is not too extravagant to define the lack of even minimal literacy, and of the cultural competence based on this foundation, as the chief obstacles to the attainment of free government in the nontechnical cultures.

2. *The Freedom of the Individual*

The human self is both unique and indubitably social. It is social in the sense that the community, beginning with the family, furnishes both the roots and the fruits of its self-fulfillment. It is unique in the sense that it has its own peculiar talents, ambitions, and sense of meaning, which no community can fully determine or control. While it needs the community for its fulfillment, it also rises indeterminately above and beyond the community to express and project its unique talents, ambitions, and its search for fulfillment, exercising its reason, imagination, and any form of cultural competence to search for meanings and purposes which may or may not be relevant to the immediate political purposes of this community. Thus cultural freedom is able to open up possibilities for the creation of transnational cultures and systems of meaning that enrich human life beyond any political purposes, either national or international.

Needless to say, the technical and cultural competence of the individual is an indispensable prerequisite for the attainment of democratic self-government. The acknowledgment of the worth of the individual and the achievement of his competence were involved in some highly contingent historical developments in the West. Fundamentally that history includes the highly contingent factor that the acknowledgment of the worth of individual selfhood preceded by centuries both the political acknowledgment of the freedom of the individual and the achievement of the technical and cultural competence to free him from organic and traditional ties and to enable him to exercise his freedom in both the economic and political sphere. In Western history the political acknowledgment of the freedom of the self had to wait upon historical developments which mitigated the undue emphasis on, and need for, social and political solidarity in the ancient and medieval world.

The religio-cultural foundations for individual selfhood which were so belatedly elaborated in the structures of free societies were laid by the Judeo-Christian faith. Unlike the mystic faiths of the Orient, it did not regard the individual and historical ego as an illusion, error, or calamity from which religion had to emancipate the self to merge it in union with the divine. On the contrary, it accepted both the self and the temporal flux in which it was imbedded as a real value and encouraged self-realization through the notion of a direct relation of the individual to the ultimate source of meaning, the divine purpose.

In the long period between the development of a religious emphasis on selfhood and its social and political fruition, the transcendent worth of the individual was both guarded and prevented from having any historical significance by the rigorous distinction made by the Church between man's "temporal" and "eternal" ends. The latter was in the keeping of the Church, while the former was involved in all manner of political and social ties under the control of traditional monarchs. Liberty meant the freedom of the Church from political control.

The medieval empires were really junior partners of the Church, which dominated the life of the Middle Ages; and the Church as Gregory VII, the founder of the medieval papacy, conceived it was ironically built on Augustinian specifications. It was the *civitas dei* of Augustine which was granted sovereignty over the "eternal" end of man.

This distinction between the political or "temporal" end and the religious or "eternal" end of man was so authoritative in the entire medieval period that when Dante's *De Monarchia* tried to rescue Christian universalism from a papal absolutism, it did not, despite his antipapalism, challenge the Church in its religious sphere. He wrote, "Let Caesar observe that reverence to Peter which the first-born son should observe to a father."[1]

Even the Reformation established liberty only in the religious sphere. Luther's conception of "evangelical liberty" left the

[1] Quoted from A. P. Entrèves, *Dante as a Political Thinker* (Oxford: Clarendon Press, 1952) , p. 58.

sovereign power of civil rulers untouched. In fact, the Reformation enhanced that power. Both Luther and Calvin were political absolutists with an extravagant reverence for political princes,
whose authority was, in their view, "God-ordained."

The emergence of the individual from the tight restrictions
and authority of the organic and political communities thus
waited upon the bourgeois period. At that time, classes possessed
the mobile and flexible forms of property, the enterprise of the
businessman and the skill of the craftsman, to pursue their own
social destiny, as well as sufficient cultural competence to articulate their desires and make their decisions in the political realm.

The bourgeois class, which achieved its triumphs in the seventeenth and eighteenth centuries, first developed in the city-states
of Italy, where it enjoyed freedom from feudal restraints. It was,
therefore, significant that the Italian Renaissance, which was
produced by the culture of the bourgeois communities, was
concerned about the freedom of the will and discussed the
relationship of such freedom to theological and natural deter-
minism in works such as Pomponazzi's *Fate, Freedom and Pre-
destination,* and Valla's *Freedom of the Will.*

The Renaissance sense of the individual was consistent in its
early and late periods. Rembrandt's late-Renaissance portraits
were the significant artistic expressions of individual uniqueness;
and Montaigne's passion for autobiography was a vivid expression of the bourgeois mood. "I present my selfe," he wrote,
"standing and lying before and behinde on the right and left
sides, and in all by natural motions.—Every man beareth the
whole stampe of humane condition."[2]

In Calvinist writings, the bourgeois sense of individual responsibility and destiny seriously challenged the religiously sanctified
political authority and claimed the right of asserting individual
decisions in political destiny. The Huguenot tract *Vindiciae
contra Tyrannos,* published in the latter part of the sixteenth

---

[2] *The Essays of Montaigne,* John Florio (trans.) (New York: E. P. Dutton,
1910), Vol. III, chaps. viii, ii.

century, succinctly stated the new political creed of the mutual covenant of justice between the ruler and the people, which sanctioned and enjoined resistance to unjust governments.

The document expressed the idea of a mutual covenant succinctly: "The people ask the King whether he will rule justly and according to the laws. The King promises he will. The people then respond that they will faithfully obey him while he governs justly. . . . If the condition is not fulfilled, the people are lawfully absolved from every obligation."[3] Thus, by a simple myth of the mutual covenant was the long reign of religiously sanctified legitimacy brought to an end, and justice rather than order became the ultimate norm of the political order.

At the end of the seventeenth century in England—after the Cromwellian protectorate had given way to the restoration of monarchy, and parliament had asserted its authority over the monarchy by an act which gave the throne to William and Mary in the interest of ensuring a Protestant succession—John Locke published a theory of community and government by covenant which gave an extravagant account of communal processes in which bourgeois voluntarism and individualism were expressed so consistently that both the organic and the collective factors of community were obscured. Locke wrote: "For, when any number of men have, by the consent of every individual, made a community, they have thereby made that community one body, with a power to act as one body, which is only by the will and determination of the majority."[4]

Thus Locke, celebrated in democratic history as the spiritual father of democratic liberties, contrived succinctly to express a very contingent element in the history of Western democracy, namely the extravagant individualism and voluntarism of the bourgeois founders of free government. This extravagance was creative in freeing the individual of the restraints of the organic,

---

[3] *"Vindiciae contra Tyrannos,"* in Francis W. Coker, *Readings in Political Philosophy* (New York: Macmillan, 1938) , p. 357.

[4] John Locke, *Two Treatises of Civil Government,* Second Treatise, chap. viii, para. 96.

traditional communities of the past ages. It was, however, a source of great hazard to the democratic cause, for it prevented bourgeois democracy from coming to terms with the collective realities of an industrial civilization. Free government in the West was in fact so tardy in devising adequate equilibriums of power to guarantee justice in the power realities of modern industrialism that it furnished real grievances which encouraged the Marxist rebellion of the industrial workers against individualistic democracy.

Fortunately, the virtues of Western democracy, including the freedom to criticize its original presuppositions and the capacity to encourage, however reluctantly, the rise of new centers of political and economic power (in this case, the trade-union movement), gave Western democracy the resources to correct early mistakes and to eliminate the injustices of early industrialism. For this reason Western democracy has proved to be more immune to the Communist virus than any other form of government. The "crisis" for which the Marxist apocalypse was intended has failed to materialize.

This summary of the course of Western democracy serves to raise questions about the presence or absence in non-European cultures of two resources of individual freedom. They may lack both the original religio-cultural foundations for an appreciation of the worth of human selfhood and the later bourgeois social and political affirmation of the individual, his emancipation from the organic, traditional cohesiveness of the older cultures. The absence, in the new nations, of the religious and social factors that initiated and elaborated individual freedom in Western culture does not make the cause of democracy hopeless in the present global situation, but it does suggest that free government is not a simple option for the new nations.

But since the extravagant Western bourgeois sense of the individual seems to obscure organic and collective aspects of human existence, it is relevant to inquire in what sense the appreciation of the worth of the individual is universally normative, even though we are aware of the contingent factors in the recognition of that worth in Western history. The genuine values of individualism which must be treasured despite Western extravagances may be briefly defined. These values exist in three categories. The first guards the security of the individual against political hysteria and chicanery and against the arbitrary exercise of power against his liberties. This value is preserved primarily in a free judicial system in which the individual finds his security even against the power of a reigning government. A trial by a jury of his peers is the historic symbol of individual security in Western history. The purge trials of Stalinist Russia are vivid reminders of the peril to individual rights in a judicial system under political domination.

The second category of normative individual rights which transcends the contingencies of Western history pertains to the right and the competence of the individual to exercise his suffrage, to have an ultimate veto power over the policies and identities of his rulers, and to give personal expression of his choices. Modern technical collectivism has seriously limited the exercise of individual freedom, particularly in the economic sphere. But this residual political freedom is a *sine qua non* of a free society, for without it communities become subject to an irresponsible oligarchy, whether of priests, commissars, or technocrats. We can no longer take for granted that this right will be exercised by dispassionate and disinterested electors, but we know that there is more security in the competition of their prejudices than in a monopoly of power exercised by any elite.

Naturally a viable democracy presupposes the intellectual competence of the voter, that he will have the ability to guard and cherish common interests of the community, above and beyond the parochial economic, ethnic, and other interests which divide the community. Without this competence and common loyalty free governments cannot be rendered viable.

The third category of individual freedoms, which might be regarded as universally normative, does not pertain to the political order. It consists in the competent expression and projection of systems of meaning and value which enrich the whole culture though they may be irrelevant, or even dangerous, to a regnant political regime. This form of individual freedom which encourages prophets, artists, and scholars enriches a whole culture within and above the political realm, and also prevents the simplification of life into a purely political mold. The young intellectuals of Communist states are now in the process of asserting this cultural freedom against the restrictions of the canons of "socialist realism," which compel the artist to extol the triumphs and virtues of the political regime. Obviously this form of freedom is difficult to achieve and preserve under an oligarchy holding a monopoly of power. It may or may not be attainable in many of the new nations, whether Communist or not. Yet it is a form of freedom without which even the most efficient technocracy is reduced to cultural barbarism.

3. *Justice and an Equilibrium of Power*

Since communities are composed of classes and other groups, and since the ultimate power of the vote is exercised by individuals who are actuated by various forms of group interests, it is obvious that the political franchise is not merely an instrument of pure and disinterested intelligence. Free communities do not merely derive the authority of government from "the consent of the governed." They represent a free and fluid competition and adjustment of group interests informed by economic and ethnic motives and loyalties. Since all convictions in the political realm are tainted by interest and are not amenable to pure reason, it follows that politics is a realm of power and interest more than of reason.

Traditional communities throughout history have sacrificed justice to order through the excessive use of power. They have tended to use sovereign power excessively because the unity of the community was never secure. Sovereign power, essentially the authority to speak and act for the community, was derived from a religiously sanctified legitimacy. The functional power of certain groups was also excessive because the priests, soldiers, and landlords enjoyed excessive prestige compared with the peasants, who had no competence beyond the limits of manual labor.

In traditional communities, functional power was related to sovereign political power. The priests and soldiers were the first, and the more significant, wielders of functional power. Both classes were quasi-sovereign in the sense that they could use force on behalf of and in the name of the community.

The Marxist interpretation of the beginning of inequality through the "division of labor" was correct except that it interpreted that division in the light of the realities of a late commercial period. The division of labor in traditional societies began much earlier; the priests and soldiers were the original beneficiaries of this division, deriving excessive benefits from their functions because they participated in sovereign power and because their ability and their functions exceeded by far those of the tillers of the land.

Our summary has revealed that the attainment of greater social justice proceeded in two steps. The first one was the rise of free government, and the second the achievement of an equilibrium of economic power within the confines of free institutions. Now we must assess the relation of the contingent factors in Western history to what may be regarded as universally relevant factors in the achievement of an equilibrium of power adequate for the achievement of justice.

The first step in the attainment of an adequate equilibrium of power was, of course, the organization of democratic societies deriving the authority of government from the consent of the governed. If history were merely governed by pure theory, one might regard the birth of democracy in the pure Lockean terms of individual choice and social contract. But history is fashioned by a clash and competition of powers which are armed with ideas related to interests but frequently and fortunately also creative

for the community as a whole. In terms of power realities the
birth of democracy can be explained as a middle-class rebellion
against the feudal order.

The middle classes, roughly the commercial groups and the
craftsmen, had become stronger with each passing century of the
Middle Ages. But neither their economic power nor their political
power was commensurate with their functional importance. Economically they were at the mercy of the mercantilism of the
traditional states which gave special privileges to the politically
powerful feudal lords entrenched in governmental power. Political power was the monopoly of the landed aristocracy, operating
under the aegis of a monarchy ruling the nation by religiously
sanctioned legitimacy. The structure of the "oppressor state" was
simple. One class presumed to speak for the whole nation. The
commercial class, the craftsmen, and the peasants were "subjects."

The peasants rebelled periodically against the gross inequalities of the traditional order, but they were weak in functional
power and had neither the economic power nor the cultural
competence to challenge the feudal lords. Thus, the rebellion
against monarchism and feudalism waited upon the development
of classes with sufficient resources to mount such a challenge and
with valid reasons for seeking a radical change in the power
structure. The most obvious reason was that the middle classes
lacked political power commensurate with their growing economic strength. The only method of changing the political
power structure was by substituting the principle of consent of
the governed for the traditional principle of legitimacy.

Our summary of Western history has revealed the many historical contingencies which were involved in the birth and
growth of democracy in the West. It includes the breakdown of
the traditional order in France and the French Revolution, the
gradual growth of the authority of parliaments and the development of constitutional monarchies in Britain, Scandinavia, and
Holland, as well as the American democratic experience, in

which national independence and constitutional government were won in the same rebellion.

Two aspects of the new power structure created by democracies must be considered. The first is the reduced power of the military class, though free societies did not eliminate the role of the defense establishments in the external affairs of the nation and did not change the essential power of the political authority to use force in behalf of the unity of the community. They did, however, subject the military to civil authority, and the free play of competitive striving in a free society reduced the necessity of using physical coercion in the interest of internal order. The military was therefore subjected to, and rigorously distinguished from, the civil authority, which was the ultimate power in the state.

The result of this subordination of military power to civil authority was to eliminate the military oligarchy as an important part of the power structure in free societies. This is an aspect of the democratic power structure in the West which many of the new nations are unable to match, since many of them owe their existence to wars of liberation, and their domestic affairs are characterized by frequent internal rebellions. The relative effectiveness of the middle class and the military in the West in replacing the old feudalism with a new power structure has created a great chasm of historical contingency between the West and the new nations in this respect.

The second significant aspect of the power structure of free societies pertains to the relation between political and economic power or between sovereign and functional power. Since the commercial classes used their growing economic power to achieve political power, there was a general tendency to assume that modern democratic communities had reversed the relation of the two forms of power and that economic power predominated. The industrial revolution gave additional credence to this belief, since the middle classes, now the industrial owners, used the power of the state in their favor and to the disadvantage of the industrial workers. Thus Communist theory, borrowing from liberal theory, simply described the "bourgeois" state as a class instrument of oppression and many of the realities of early industrialism seemed to justify this indictment.

But the second phase of the industrial revolution refuted the indictment and thereby threw light on the relation between economic and political, between functional and sovereign power. For in the second stage of the Industrial Revolution, the workers achieved the right to organize and bargain collectively.

Although the workers possessed the political power inherent in the franchise, it was not enough. They were worsted in the functional or economic realm in which the modern machine transferred the tools and the skills of the old craftsman to the factory. This created a radical disequilibrium of power which was not corrected until the workers achieved the right to bargain collectively.

It is significant that the establishment of an equilibrium of power in the economic realm enabled the sovereign power of the state to validate itself as an instrument of justice for all classes. Thus a free society could prove itself in sufficient possession of sovereign power to govern a nation, preserve its unity, and prevent the disaffection of a disinherited minority by borrowing from the equilibrium of functional power in the economic sphere in order to enhance its sovereign power. Sovereign power is always the authority to speak and act for the community, and in a free society that authority rests upon the prestige of its ability to establish justice rather than a coerced order.

If we seek to distinguish between the factors contingent to Western history and the basic norm relevant for all communities, which is that there must be a tolerable equilibrium of power for the sake of a tolerable justice, we come to the conclusion that an industrial civilization is more able to establish such an equilibrium than an agrarian culture, but that it can do so only after a strong class of organized workers is able to create a balance of power with the owners and managers of the industrial enterprise.

Non-European states do not have to imitate all the contingencies of Western history, but the evidence reveals that it is difficult to preserve democracy without an adequate internal equilibrium of power.

An analysis of sovereign, or political, power and of functional, or economic, power would seem inadequate without a reference to property, which both the liberal and the Marxist theories regard as the very core of economic power. But such theories obscure the subordinate nature of property in the realm of functional power. Significantly, both the Communist states and the democratic (capitalist) states have elaborated managerial forms of power which reveal that property is not the primary source of economic power. Adolf Berle, in his *Power Without Property,* has analyzed the course of the diffusion of property in industrial establishments through the diffusion of stock owner-ship, thus leaving the significant power in the hands of the managers. The Communists have, of course, socialized property, and their managerial class has become strictly subordinate to the political oligarchy, refuting in Communist practice the Marxist theory of the dominance of economic power.

II

The Prospects for
Democracy in the
Developing Areas

6

AFRICA: TRIBALISM, THE ONE-PARTY STATE, AND THE RISE OF THE MILITARY

I N THE PRECEDING CHAPTERS we have seen that free government developed in the West only in a particular environment and under a particular set of conditions. It presupposed the establishment of national unity with a common adherence to a set of national symbols. These symbols provided the social cement to replace, or at least to compete successfully with, the more fundamental pre-existing loyalties to subnational or supranational groups. Aided by an increase in literacy and the economic advances of the commercial middle classes, the philosophy of individualism and liberty finally triumphed in Europe, giving political application to beliefs which had long been part of the

Judeo-Christian tradition. An independent judiciary, religious, cultural, and political pluralism, and the establishment of democratic legitimacy through competitive elections opened up the possibilities for the accession of new groups to political influence and ultimately resulted in the emergence of a political equilibrium among competing groups capable of producing a tolerable approach to social justice in an atmosphere of freedom. The earlier domination of the military, religious, and landowning elites gave way to the rise of commercial and middle classes, and later the political system was also able to incorporate the legitimate demands of the workers and the small farmers. The individualist self-assertion necessary to break down older organic and corporate ties was sometimes carried to excess both in ideology and practice. Yet the free governments in the West retained a flexibility and openness to criticism and change which permitted them to adjust to the new collective requirements of the welfare-oriented bureaucratic superstate while maintaining a concern for the protection of individual liberty and the free activity of groups within the state.

This evolution took place over many centuries and with no necessary inevitability about the pattern of its development. In some countries the balance of social forces left some groups without political influence. In others, economic depression, political defeat, and the incompetence of democratic leadership permitted individuals or groups opposed to freedom to take power. And in many countries the full implication of the democratic ideal of equality is still to be realized for some minority groups.

Two particular factors have been involved in the emergence of nations committed to free government and social justice in the West. On the one hand, the spread of literacy made it possible to establish the communications necessary for the development of national loyalties, belief in individual ability and worth, and demands for a sharing of power by less privileged groups. On the other, the unprecedented economic expansion of Europe gave rulers the economic means to establish strong nation-states, and fostered the development of new centers of economic power demanding recognition by appealing to a philosophy of liberal individualism which both impeded and permitted the recognition of additional group demands in later centuries. Without shattering national unity, the political community was broadened to include new groups, such as farmers, workers, ethnic minorities, and the poor, permitting them to influence and alter national policy in favor of their legitimate claims. In no case has the process been completely successful, and only a tolerable approach to justice has been achieved, but it has progressed sufficiently to maintain confidence in the ability of free government in the West to offer its citizens order, justice, and social welfare.

When we turn to Africa, Asia, the Middle East, and Latin America and inquire about the relevance of the history of the development of free government in the West to the emergence of similar regimes in the developing areas, we are faced with dramatic contrasts between the European and North American experience and the present and past politics and economics of most of the rest of the globe. For many of the developing states, nationhood is a fragile achievement only recently acquired and continually challenged by regional, ethnic, economic, religious, or tribal loyalties which threaten national cohesion.

The new nations have been recognized internationally, but domestically a sense of national unity and loyalty has yet to be developed in many of them, and, even in those which have long existed, a sense of nationhood has not taken root except among an urbanized elite. Massive illiteracy makes politicization difficult, and underdevelopment, in which a large sector of the national economy is devoted to subsistence agriculture, keeps major segments of the population out of any meaningful contact with national and international life. Organic communities, especially the "extended-family" system, make it difficult for a sense of individual responsibility and achievement to develop, and the basis for the national articulation and integration of individual and group interests is lacking. When the experiment of democracy is tried, it only reinforces the divisions in the society, and often it breaks down from the lack of a general will among squabbling, opportunistic, and often venal representatives of the people. Where Christianity is the dominant religion, it frequently takes authoritarian and submissive forms that contrast with the more individualistic Christianity, both Protestant and Roman Catholic, of northern Europe and the United States. In fact, if one looks at the developing areas in terms of the conditions outlined above, it appears that the prospects of responsible self-government are very dim indeed. Yet in some cases a form of democracy has endured and even prospered, suggesting that in terms of the above analysis one may legitimately ask not why has democracy failed in many of the developing countries but rather why has it succeeded in any of them.

Africa seems to typify dramatically the problems for the emergence of free government in less developed areas. The economic and political expansion of Europe between the fifteenth and nineteenth centuries brought all but a small part of Africa (Liberia and Ethiopia) under colonial control, and by the twentieth century forces had been set in motion which ultimately led to the emergence of the independent states of that continent. At first, European religion and later (and to a much lesser extent) European education were extended to Africans, and the ideological and intellectual weapons which were to forge African independence were placed in the hands of a small, Western-educated elite. During and after World War II, the British established the beginnings of a native administration and national parliamentary institutions in Ghana and Nigeria which, it was hoped, would survive the transition to independence. Somewhat later, France, seeing the handwriting on the wall, began to train an African political elite by educating the ablest young Africans in French universities and by bringing African politicians into the French political system. Belgium tried another approach. After establishing a broad primary-school system in the Congo, the Belgians hoped to be able to forestall demands for greater autonomy or independence by restricting admission to secondary schools and practically barring entrance to the university. All of these strategies were implemented through colonial structures whose outlines conformed to the interests and needs of the colonizers and had little relation to pre-existing patterns of African tribal and ethnic loyalties. It is true that the British made frequent use of the tribal leaders as instruments of "indirect rule," but the geographic contours of their colonies did not coincide with tribal divisions. The geographic divisions had been established for the most part at the Berlin Conference in 1884–85 by diplomats with little knowledge of Africa.

Yet when independence did come to Africa, it was these artificially created colonies which were granted the status of independent nations. They were endowed with representative legislatures, political parties, elections, and all the trappings of Western free government. The basis of legitimacy was to be majority rule and minority rights; the institutions of government were to be modeled on those of Western Europe. The picture in *Life* magazine at the time of the independence of Ghana in 1957 showing a bewigged African speaker presiding over a replica of the House of Parliament, with Government and Opposition facing one another in solemn array, symbolized the hopes of the colonizers for a transfer of democratic institutions to the former colonies. Yet within a few years, the English wigs gave way to African tribal symbols, the shape of the parliament was changed to a semicircle, and the leaders of the opposition were in jail. The oratory of the Ghanaian leader, Kwame Nkrumah, and the repressive laws which were enacted in Accra persuaded Western observers that a totalitarian state was replacing what had promised to be a model of British-style democracy in Africa. Then, with little warning, the incipient dictator was overthrown by the army in February, 1966, and the regalia of the former regime were revealed to be an elaborate façade behind which nothing had really changed since independence except the scale of corruption of the politicians. Behind the game of democracy and totalitarianism being played in Accra were the changeless rhythm of village life, a decentralized and segmented tribal society, and the continued dependence of Ghana on the fluctuating world cocoa market. The creation of what appeared to be a mass party, the Convention People's Party, and Nkrumah's great schemes for industrialization had not fundamentally altered the political and economic reality, nor had they moved Ghana much closer to modernization. As of this writing, the military government in Accra has asked for civilian assistance in establishing a system which will once again apply the Western liberal norms of free elections, constitutional restraints, and a partially competitive economy, and hopes for the eventual emergence of free government in Ghana have been raised once more.

In the Ghanaian case, it is easy to attribute the failure of parliamentary government to the megalomania of one man, but it must be recognized that the tribal problem was also involved. The Ashanti nation around Kumasi in central Ghana had always opposed Nkrumah, who was not an Ashanti, and tribal chiefs throughout Ghana were reluctant to surrender their power to an upstart without traditional authority. The cult of personality which Nkrumah built up around himself was at least in part an attempt to borrow the trappings of a traditional chief (the ceremonies of the central government were consciously modeled on tribal rites) and to outshine them in splendor and appeal. Nkrumah then went on to label anyone who opposed him as a tribalist, including the Ghanaian middle class and professionals in Accra who had originated the nationalist movement. He was partially successful in his efforts to establish himself as supreme ruler, but he failed to reckon with the army, which was shocked by the corruption and irrationality of his regime. The army also held a near monopoly of the instruments of coercion, and when Nkrumah threatened this monopoly by his plan to establish a popular militia, it moved against him.

In the other model British colony in West Africa, Nigeria, tribalism contributed more directly to the collapse of what had appeared to be a model of democratic federalism. When Nigeria became independent in 1961, it was divided into three regions, in each of which one tribal group and one political party were dominant. In the North, the Muslim Hausa leaders had organized the Northern People's Congress. In the East, the Ibos were the dominant group in the National Council of Nigeria and the Cameroons (NCNC), while in the West, the Yoruba leaders belonged to the Action Group. After independence, attempts were made by each of these groups and parties to move into the territory of the other. In the North they were unsuccessful, since the tight control of the Muslim leaders prevented any incursion of southern parties. When the leader of the Action Group, Abafemi Awolowo, found himself in opposition to an alliance of the Northern People's Congress and the NCNC, he recast his ideology in a more radical form in order to appeal to the NCNC's left wing. The NCNC in turn encouraged a split in the Action Group, and the central government was able to discover first, massive corruption in the Western Region, and shortly thereafter evidence of subversion carried on by Action Group leaders. However, tribally based loyalties to the imprisoned leaders continued to disturb the Western Region, and when the elections there were blatantly rigged in 1964 and 1965, rioting broke out. In January, 1966, a group of military conspirators sympathetic to the radical nationalism of the imprisoned Action Group leaders overthrew and killed the heads of the federal and regional governments. For a time, they were outmaneuvered by General Aguiye-Ironsi, who took over the government in the name of national unity. Yet within six months, another coup had taken place, an orgy of murder of southern Ibos swept through the North, and shortly thereafter the Federation of Nigeria began to break up. If Nigeria survives its current bloody civil war, it will still have to come to terms with the reality of tribalism, the effects of which on the Nigerian experiment in federal democracy can only be described as disastrous.

Previously it had been hoped that the balance of forces among the Nigerian tribal groups might provide the basis for pluralistic democracy, compelling them to form a coalition government and to tolerate the opposition. Instead, the deep-seated hatred between the Hausa of the North and the Ibo of the East has divided Nigeria, perhaps irrevocably.

The secession of the Eastern Region as Biafra, like the earlier secession of Katanga in the Congo, suggests that tribalism is more likely to lead to anarchy than to pluralism, unless broader loyalties are developed by education and national leadership. The Biafran case is more agonizing for the partisans of modernization and development, since the Ibos were the most enterprising and democratic group in the Federation of Nigeria and the suffering they underwent provides considerable justification for secession. At the same time, the discovery of considerable oil deposits in the East has created an additional incentive for the Ibos to go it alone rather than be subordinated to a numerically dominant but backward Hausa majority within the Nigerian Federation.

Yet the secession of Biafra could provide a precedent for similar tribally based movements elsewhere and lead to the creation of further "ministates" in a continent which already suffers from an excess of Balkanization. A compromise solution involving the further decentralization of the power of the federal government is also not acceptable to those in power in Lagos, since it would leave the oil revenues in the hands of the regional government. Yet a solution based on indefinite military occupation of the region seems no more satisfactory. Democratic theory provides no clear guidelines for this type of problem, since there is no indication as to the appropriate unit of political organization or the proper division of powers between the center and the federal units.

Other examples could be cited of the failure of federal structures to solve the problem of tribalism in Africa. In the former British protectorate of Uganda, the special position and privileges of the Buganda people could not survive the first disagreement after independence, when the Premier, Milton Obote, found it necessary to abolish the constitutional guarantees of autonomy for the Buganda area. In the neighboring state of Kenya, tribalism has had an opposite effect, since there it operated to guarantee a territorial base for the leaders of the Kenya People's Union when they seceded from Jomo Kenyatta's Kenya African National Union. Their secession was based on ideological differences, but those who were successful in retaining their parliamentary seats in the elections which followed owed their success to tribalism, not ideology.

Unlike West Africa, East Africa's problems in establishing national unity and basic consensus are complicated by the existence of sizable non-African minorities. The white settler problem which loomed so large in Kenyan politics before independence seems less serious today, but the position of the Indian small businessmen and traders remains precarious throughout East Africa. In Rhodesia and South Africa, of course, the dominance of the large European minority has been assured by law, and the prospects for democratic self-government on the basis of majority rule and minority rights is at present very remote. Racial divisions have seemed a less serious problem in Tanzania, due to the multiplicity of tribes and the small size of racial minorities, yet when President Julius Nyerere introduced electoral competition into Tanzania's single-party system, ethnic and religious factors were found to be important in electoral success.[1]

Probably the most striking example of the threat of tribalism to national unity has been furnished in the Congo. Given independence before a party system or national leadership had been allowed to develop, the Congo was quickly divided into tribal fiefdoms under the leadership of opportunistic leaders, and only the action of the United Nations, and later of a weak Congolese Army, succeeded in maintaining a semblance of national unity. Crawford Young, in *Politics in the Congo,* has observed that the politics of ethnicity is not a uniquely Congolese or African problem. He has even used the term "cultural pluralism" rather than

[1] See Lionel Cliffe (ed.) , *One Party Democracy: The 1965 Tanzania General Elections* (Nairobi, Kenya: East African Publishing House, 1967) .

tribalism, so as to emphasize the resemblances to similar political problems elsewhere. However, the difference between the Congolese situation and that in most other countries in which there are politically relevant ethnic divisions lies in the absence of an accepted central authority and a national loyalty transcending and mediating tribal differences.

The example of the Congo may also be used to qualify our earlier assertion concerning the need for widespread literacy as a prerequisite for the establishment of national unity. Congolese literacy figures were higher than those of most of the other states of tropical Africa (before independence nearly one-third of the children of primary-school age were attending school), but Belgian policy had restricted education almost exclusively to the primary-school level, and the first Congolese to seek higher education in Europe left the Congo only four years before independence. As the lack of qualified native leaders after independence demonstrated, not only is a minimal level of literacy needed for a real democracy, but there must also be an educated and sophisticated national elite to lead the country. Sometimes this education and political sophistication can be acquired in other ways than through formal schooling (as in the case of Sekou Touré of Guinea, who received his political education in the trade-union movement), but a national view of politics, some understanding of international relations, and a minimal technical competence in handling the instruments of government are prerequisites for the exercise of power. African leaders who lack these must rely on outside forces and powers and postpone the day when real self-government can be attained.

Recognizing that literacy is a prerequisite for the creation of nationhood, all the new African nations have set up crash programs to expand their educational facilities. The mission schools which in many areas had a monopoly on education have been brought under national control, and the curriculums have been reorganized to give them a nationalistic flavor. On this level, however, the line between education and indoctrination is not very clear, and the question remains whether the new educational programs will develop responsible citizens or passive political tools. The expansion of opportunities on the secondary level (the real bottleneck), and the increase in African universities and in overseas scholarships are encouraging signs for the future development of a political, scientific, and technical elite which can provide the social basis for diffusion of power and responsible self-government. Because of the critical shortage of educated university graduates in Africa, there seems less likelihood of the development of a frustrated intellectual proletariat like that of India or of alienated revolutionary student groups along Latin American lines. While it is fashionable for African students in London or Paris to adopt a revolutionary Marxist position, their almost total dependence on existing African governments for scholarship support as students and for employment thereafter works to diminish their revolutionary fervor and to incorporate them into the system.

Democratic theorists from John Stuart Mill to Seymour M. Lipset have discussed the educational prerequisites for democratic government. Literacy tests exist in many developed countries, but the spread of primary education has meant that they do not exclude large segments of the population. In the newly independent African countries, however, where literacy rates range from 1 per cent (Mozambique) to 37.5 per cent (the Congo), such tests would exclude most of the population. Moreover, since literacy tests had earlier been used to exclude the black majority from power, it has been politically impossible to suggest any formula other than "one man, one vote." Studies of African elections have shown that it is possible to conduct elections among illiterates by the use of symbols, etc., but the question of how much these elections have meant in the way of meaningful choice or influence on government policy remains open.[2]

Elections are less significant today in most African countries because they are governed by one-party or military regimes. In one African country—Tanzania—a more meaningful electoral

[2] See T. E. Smith, *Elections in Developing Countries* (New York and London: St. Martins Press, 1960).

choice was made possible within a one-party regime, when the regulations for the parliamentary elections of September, 1965, provided for two candidates for every parliamentary seat (although there was only one candidate for the Presidency, Julius Nyerere). Both candidates, however, had to be approved by the district and national organizations of the party. Nonetheless, the competitive element did increase the responsiveness of the representatives to their constituents' needs, although irrational factors such as the position on the ballot or the symbol used for the candidate also played a significant role.[3] One might conclude from this example that literacy is not a requirement for the expression of immediate grievances and needs but that illiteracy makes a reasoned choice between candidates much more difficult. (This is not to be taken as an assertion that literacy alone will guarantee the rational quality of an electoral decision, but only that it may make it more likely.)

Some African countries are exceptions to the rule of one-party or military governments. The Sudan held free elections in 1964 (except in the South, where disturbed conditions made elections impossible). Morocco, Madagascar, Kenya, Zambia, and Somalia have opposition parties with representatives in parliament, and local elections were contested in Uganda even after the Obote anti-Buganda coup. The new South African states of Botswana, Lesotho, and Swaziland have also held free elections, but, in view of the overwhelming majorities won by one party in Botswana and Swaziland, there is some doubt about the continuation of competitive politics there. (In Lesotho, the opposition party has had legal difficulties, but the government has specifically rejected the one-party alternative.) The list of constitutional democracies in Africa is not a long one, and it is likely to grow even shorter in the future.

The economic situation in most African countries does not

[3] See Lionel Cliffe (ed.), *op. cit.*, and Henry Bienen, *Tanzania, Party Transformation and Economic Development* (Princeton, N.J.: Princeton University Press, 1967).

appear to offer an encouraging prospect for the development of free government. The growth rates of some African states (e.g. Gabon, the Ivory Coast, Liberia, and Mauritania) are among the highest in the world, but this is partly because the starting point is so low, and the favorable political effects of this economic growth are minimized when the benefits go principally to foreign investors and a few politicians and bureaucrats. Lacking a domestic base for capital formation, development is dependent on foreign aid or overseas investment, and Soviet, American, and French aid to Africa has declined in recent years while private investment has been concentrated in certain particularly advantageous areas. It has shunned the more radical regimes such as Algeria, Mali, and Guinea, where the economic decline is particularly evident today. In some cases windfall earnings based on sudden increases in the price of certain primary products have brought a short-term increase in the gross national product. The reverse, however, has also taken place, e.g., the drop in the price of cocoa, which has severely affected the balance of payments of Ghana and other African cocoa producers. While Africa's population growth is not as great as that of Asia and Latin America, it has nullified and in some cases (1965–66, for example) overtaken the annual rate of increase of agricultural production, indicating that a food-production crisis may possibly arise.

So far there is little evidence of the emergence of economic interest groups as a limit on those which wield political power. Ghana under Nkrumah made some efforts to organize the farmers into an interest group, but this was done for purposes of state control rather than political representation. Before independence, the trade unions played an important political role in Morocco, Tunisia, Guinea, Kenya, and Tanganyika, and at various times since independence they have been of some significance in Nigeria, Ghana, Upper Volta, and the Congo (Brazzaville), but the tendency in most African countries has been to limit the power of the unions, since it is likely to be exerted principally to extract higher wages from an economy in which the organized worker already enjoys a privileged position in comparison with the rest of the population.

Because commerce and business in Africa frequently are in the hands of foreigners, they do not provide a base for the expression of political pluralism and emergent self-government. It is true that the interests of the foreign investors and governments must be considered by political decision-makers, but this does not promote the kind of domestic economic pluralism in which Africans themselves influence and restrain their governments. Moreover, foreign economic interests offer a ready target for political demagoguery, and by helping to divert attention from the inadequacy or corruption of the political leaders, provide a convenient scapegoat for the failure to achieve the hoped-for levels of economic development. In countries like Ghana and Nigeria, however, there is an African professional class with a commitment to European liberal ideals; in Ghana, this group has re-emerged after its eclipse in the waning days of the Nkrumah regime. In addition, there is also an important group of petty traders and market women who can be a political force.

The significant economic activity, however, in most African states either rests in the hands of the government or is subject to government control and regulation (e.g., the substantial foreign investments in areas such as Zambia, Katanga, Liberia, and the Ivory Coast). Despite their nearly unanimous commitment to "African socialism," there has been little nationalization in Africa since independence (Guinea, Algeria, Mali, Tanzania, and the United Arab Republic are the only examples that come to mind), but the influence of government policy on the modernized part of the economy is so great that there is little opportunity for the development of a relatively independent private sector able to provide an alternative base for the development of leadership skills and criticism of government policy—as well as an alternative occupation for those not involved in government. The economic rewards of the public sector are so much greater than those of other parts of the economy that politics has become a much more brutal struggle than in societies in which other alternatives are available and where an expanding economy moderates the intensity of competition for political power. In addition, the influence of the government in the economy and the absence of effective political criticism combine to produce a situation that invites the kind of corruption and influence-peddling which has characterized so many African governments since independence and has provided the single most compelling inducement and justification for the wave of military coups which has swept Africa.

To continue to offer the people the possibility of choosing other policies and leadership requires political and economic self-restraint on the part of those in power. This restraint is difficult to achieve without the development of institutions which reinforce personal conscience in discouraging the abuse of power. The Western liberal tradition, which grew out of the effort to limit the power of monarchs and landowning aristocrats, has emphasized (perhaps overemphasized) the dangers inherent in the exercise of power, and only recently has it come to realize the positive good that can be accomplished by the responsible use of the resources of government. The new African states suffer from the opposite defect—an excessive optimism about the possibilities of political change through the exercise of governmental power. Institutionalized limits on power are seen as threats to the attempt to build a new nation, and the existence of opposing groups appears much more dangerous when the consensus on new institutions is fragile and unstable. The result in many African states (and not only those which appear to be pursuing more radical policies internationally) has been an attempt to control potential centers of criticism and opposition, such as trade unions, youth organizations, student groups, the press, the judiciary, and the bureaucracy. This control has been defended in a theory of one-party democracy which, by combining the populism of Rousseau with the Leninist theory of imperialist neo-colonialism, insists on the identity of the popular will with that

of the ruling elite and associates all opposition with the maneu-
vers and intrigues of foreign powers.[4]

To the outside observer it sometimes appears that Africa is
ruled by petty totalitarian dictators who mouth the slogans of
democracy to conceal their own interests in power and corruption. Yet a closer look at the individual regimes reveals a wide
variety among them, and none of them approach the rigidity of a
police state or totalitarian regime. The Tanzanian example of
competitive elections within a one-party regime has already been
discussed; Algeria tried the same system in its municipal elections
in 1967; and other regimes do more than merely pay lip service
to their commitment to free discussion and compromise before
reaching decisions within the party—at least among the party
leadership. The Kenyan example already mentioned also raises
the possibility that the nationalist parties may undergo a process
of splitting-off over policy differences, such as that which took
place in India's Congress Party before and after independence.
One observer has seen the development of interest group representation within the Tunisian Destour Socialist Party as a hope-
ful augury for the future of constitutionalism.[5] On a longer-range
view, one can foresee the emergence of additional politically
conscious groups and individuals who will demand that attention
be paid to their needs. The problem in the future is more likely
to be the instability that results from the incapacity of the government to satisfy those demands than the rigidity and imposed
conformity that results from a totalitarian regime.

This prognosis is reinforced when one observes the relative
weakness of the new government structures in Africa, and the

4 See the selections by Sekou Touré, Madeira Keita, Kwame Nkrumah, and
Julius Nyerere in Paul E. Sigmund (ed.), *The Ideologies of the Developing
Nations* (rev. ed.; New York: Frederick A. Praeger, 1967).

5 Clement Moore, "Tunisia After Bourguiba: Liberalization or Political
Degeneration?" paper delivered at Princeton University Conference, March
24, 1966, as well as his "Mass Party Regimes in Africa," in Herbert J.
Spiro (ed.), *Africa: The Primacy of Politics* (New York: Random House,
1966), and "The Neo-Destour, a Structure for Democracy?" *World Politics*,
XIV (October, 1961), pp. 467–82.

almost total breakdown in many areas of the party organizations that led the fight for independence. As the most able party leaders become involved in central government administration and policy, local and regional party organizations are manned by less qualified personnel, or they simply cease to function. This phenomenon, described by Africanists as the emergence of the "no-party state," was most evident in the Congo, where the parties that had sprung up before independence degenerated into parliamentary cliques without any roots in the country. Thus the rhetoric about mobilizing the country for development might simply serve to conceal the absence of a political machine to carry out the plans of the leadership in the capital.[6] The problem then of free government in Africa consists in avoiding both the extremes of repression and anarchy. To have free government, one must first have government. To have political liberty, one must first have a political community.

Some apologists for the single-party system maintain that it is just as free and democratic as the two-party and multiparty systems in other parts of the world, but others are frank to admit that a certain amount of coercion is necessary at the outset in order to establish a new political community and break down the old traditional order. (Kwame Nkrumah, for example, in his *Autobiography,* speaks of the necessity of "emergency methods of a totalitarian kind" in the period following independence.) Yet the question that has been raised by Africans as well as outside observers is whether opposition and criticism will ever be allowed to emerge once a party elite is in control of the state instruments of coercion. Moreover, the experience in Ghana and elsewhere has not confirmed the claims of the defenders of the one-party state that it would bring political stability and rapid economic development, and the single party does not now receive the unanimous support in Africa which it enjoyed at the time of

6 On this, see David Hapgood, *Africa: From Independence to Tomorrow* (New York: Atheneum, 1965) and Aristide Zolberg, *Creating Political Order: The Party States of West Africa* (Chicago: Rand McNally, 1966) .

independence.[7] Still it must be admitted that the argument that in a traditional society, democracy can sometimes be an obstacle to modernization is not without some basis in fact. If the forces of tradition and tribalism are sufficiently clever, they can manipulate democratic forms to reinforce their power and impede social and economic development, as was done in northern Nigeria before the succession of military coups described earlier.

It has been suggested that the charismatic leader can create a national consciousness and lead the people from tradition to modernity with a minimum of coercion.[8] By his prestige and appeal, the leader of the new nation can create new loyalties, establish new institutions, and integrate, modernize, or dilute the traditional authorities. (His role is not unlike that of the Lawgiver in the political thought of Plato's *Laws*, Machiavelli's *Discourses*, and Rousseau's *Social Contract*.) In Africa, charismatic figures such as Nkrumah, Sekou Touré, Julius Nyerere, or Jomo Kenyatta immediately come to mind. Yet as this list indicates, in the determination of the future evolution of new nations very much depends on the will of a single individual. The analysis of the economic, social, philosophical, and political prerequisites of free government does not perhaps give enough emphasis to the crucial role of the political leader and the values that he cherishes. The place in his personal scale of value preferences for individual and group freedoms, as compared with economic development or personal prestige and power, will have much to do with the political evolution of his country, and his concern with institution-building will determine whether the system he establishes survives him and what its characteristics will be. A figure such as Nyerere seems genuinely committed to freedom of expression and popular participation, while Nkrumah gave higher priorities to other values. (Even in Nyerere's case, the commitment to the basic values of a free society is

7 See the various opinions in Sigmund, *op. cit.*, pp. 53–56, 167–72, 183–86.
8 See, for instance, David Apter, *The Gold Coast in Transition* (Princeton, N.J.: Princeton University Press, 1955).

tempered by a concern to work out an African communitarianism which differs from what he considers the excessive individualism of the West. Moreover, the Tanzanian Government has imprisoned an estimated thirty-five enemies of the regime under its Preventive Detention Act, and Tanzanian trade unions are under tight government control.) As in so many other cases, it is often a matter of historical contingency which type of leader emerges and whether conditions will permit him to maintain himself in power.

It is also largely a matter of historical accident and individual decision whether a given country chooses the Communist path to modernization. No African country has made this decision as yet, although Zanzibar, before its federation with Tanganyika, and the Congo (Brazzaville) have come close to doing so. The Communist method offers the possibility of more rapid economic development and mobilization of the population, but African leaders have been critical of its atheism, the inapplicability of its economic analysis to the problems of Africa, and its lack of success in agriculture. Nevertheless, certain aspects of Communist theory, such as Lenin's doctrine of imperialism, have found wide acceptance in Africa, and in certain situations the Communist view of the development of African politics may coincide with that of rural traditionalists in their opposition to the Western-educated modernizing elite and produce a nativist-Communist rebellion of the type that wracked the Congo (Kinshasa) in 1965. Yet on strictly pragmatic grounds it is evident that the economic interests of Africa lie with the West, even if they reject political links through alliances or other "neocolonialist" forms of dependence. In the long run, these common interests should prevail, although the example of much of Latin America may indicate that close economic links with democratic countries in the West will not of themselves ensure or even encourage the creation or continued existence of democratic government in the countries so linked.

Recent events in Africa have suggested that a new set of political actors has emerged: the leaders of the African armies. In a political context in which there are few differentiated and self-conscious interest groups and in which disagreements over legitimacy exist, the army, even if it is as small as most African armies are, can exert a very powerful political influence if it so chooses. As Thomas Hobbes once said, where no other cards are agreed upon, clubs are trumps.[9] The first intimation of the emerging role of the African military appeared in 1963, when army dissatisfaction with low wages led to the overthrow and murder of one of the most capable African leaders, Sylvanus Olympio of Togo. In 1964, Julius Nyerere had to call in British troops to put down an army revolt in Tanganyika. Since then, the African armies have been more successful in seizing power. In recent years, armies have overthrown civilian governments in Algeria, the Congo, the Central African Republic, Dahomey (four times), Upper Volta, Nigeria, Ghana, Burundi, again in Togo, in Sierra Leone, and in Mali.

These coups were not always motivated merely by a desire for greater privileges and perquisites for the military. Often it was the incompetence and corruption of the civilian leaders which led the armies to move. The example of the breakdown of order in the Congo which was observed first-hand by Nigerian and Ghanaian officers in the United Nations Force seems to have done much to contribute to their decision to revolt against their civilian rulers. Military standards of efficiency and patriotism provided added motivation.

In the cases of Ghana and Nigeria, the army officers announced that they intended to surrender power to civilian authorities after the promulgation of a new constitution, and in the former case it was specifically stated that this constitution was to institutionalize restraints on the executive through such devices as the separation of powers and the independence of the judiciary. At the time of this writing, the army officers are still in control in

[9] Cited in Dankwart Rustow, *A World of Nations* (Washington: Brookings, 1967), p. 177.

both countries, but they have repeatedly indicated that they desire a return of democracy. In Ghana, a constitutional commission has proposed a constitution embodying the principles of separation of powers, a strictly limited executive, and a greatly strengthened judiciary with extensive powers of judicial review. In a similar development in Sierra Leone, a civilian-rule committee was appointed in January, 1968, and the apparent victor in the 1967 elections was called back to Sierra Leone and instructed to form a government which would include representatives of his political opposition.

One interesting and somewhat different example of the surrender of power to civilians by army officers has already taken place in the Sudan. In 1958, a military group removed the civilian politicians and attempted to govern the Sudan exclusively through military officers. By 1964, it had become evident that there was strong popular opposition to military rule both in the capital city and among the rebellious groups in the south. Under pressure particularly from the university students, the army officers surrendered power, and Sudan is currently governed by a multiparty, freely elected parliamentary regime. Should this regime prove unable to cope with the problems of the country, it may in turn be overthrown by the army, and we may see here a future pattern of African politics—an alternation of civilian and military elites not unlike that which has characterized many Latin American countries in recent years. (Sudan is also the only African country with a legal Communist Party, but its support is limited to university students and the capital city of Khartoum.)

In the period just after the emergence of independent Africa, the strong current favoring African unification in a Pan-African federation gave some ground for the belief that a federated Africa could provide the kind of unity in diversity that would encourage the development of free institutions on a continental level. When the Organization of African Unity was founded in 1963, it seemed to have healed the evident breach between the more radical "Casablanca" powers (Ghana, Guinea, Mali, the

United Arab Republic, Algeria, and, for a short time, Morocco) and the moderate "Monrovia" group. However, its subsequent development has demonstrated that the OAU is not likely to be more than a weak confederation with limited powers of discussion, consultation, and conciliation, rather than the strong federal political structure which the earlier Pan-Africanist writers had hoped for. The differences of political orientation persist, but the real obstacle in the way of closer ties on a Pan-African basis is the reluctance of African national leaders to surrender the pride and prestige of nationhood, however artificial some of those nations may be.

At the present time, efforts at integration have concentrated on regional units of a primarily economic nature, such as the East African Community, the Customs and Economic Union of the French-speaking states of Central Africa (UDEAC), and the Common Organization of (French-speaking) Africa and Madagascar (OCAM). To the extent that these groupings promote economic development, they may contribute to the eventual emergence of democratic government, but so far there are no signs that a common political organization will emerge on the basis of these economic ties (although the East Africans have agreed to establish a common Legislative Assembly). Even if such structures are created, there is little likelihood that they will make a significant contribution to the growth of the domestic pluralism and tolerance which form the basis of democratic government.

It is impossible to predict the future course of African politics, but the above review of the present factors operating on the emergent African systems indicates that the impediments to self-government are considerable. Socially, educationally, economically, ideologically, and politically, there seem to exist almost insuperable obstacles to the development of that balance between order and freedom which we call constitutional democracy. Yet the alternatives to democratic constitutionalism have not shown themselves superior either in creating political order

or in promoting economic development and social justice.[10] The
African continent is undergoing rapid changes and is attempting
to borrow institutions and methods from other parts of the world
and develop its own unique forms. The economic and educational modernization of many parts of the continent is breaking
down some of the most serious impediments to free government,
and the search continues for a new synthesis, which will retain
the communal, social, and cultural values of an earlier society and
still provide both the material advantages of economic development and the political values of freedom. Thus while there is no
reason to believe that African politics will duplicate the Western
pattern of political development, it is still far too early to decide
that free government has no future in Africa.

10 For examples of recent "revisionist" criticism of the apologists of authoritarianism in Africa, see W. Arthur Lewis, *Politics in West Africa* (New York:
Oxford University Press, 1965) ("The single party thus fails in all its claims.
It cannot represent all the people; or maintain free discussion; or give stable
government, or, above all, reconcile the differences between various regional
groups." [p. 63]), and Aristide Zolberg, *Creating Political Order: The
Party-States of West Africa* (Chicago: Rand McNally, 1966) ("That genuine
democracy in one of its many forms is a suitable regime for men in Africa as
elsewhere can be stated without a doubt; that the rulers of most West African
states as well as the bulk of the intellectuals deserve to be blamed for not
having tried very hard to bring about such a regime is also quite clear."
[p. 158]).

7

THE MIDDLE EAST: AUTHORITARIAN MODERNIZERS AND ISLAMIC TRADITIONALISM

IN CONTRAST TO AFRICA, nationalism has a long history in the Middle East. Yet throughout that history, Middle Eastern nationalists have had difficulty defining the precise geographic limits of the nation to which they want to give their loyalties. For the Pan-Arab movement, it is a union of the Arabic-speaking peoples of the Middle East, but until now internal rivalries and external intervention have frustrated progress toward Arab unity. For others, Islam must form the unifying bond of a Pan-Arab nation. But an Islamic nation would exclude Lebanon, which has a small Christian majority, as well as Christian minorities in other countries, such as the 4 million Copts in Egypt.

Moreover, some Middle Eastern countries have national traditions which would resist incorporation into a larger Arab or Muslim union. Turkey, for example, although overwhelmingly Muslim in religion, has chosen to remain apart from Middle Eastern politics. The picture is further complicated by the existence of groups like the Kurds in Iraq and Turkey who would like to see new nations carved out of those which exist today.

All of this demonstrates that our first condition for the development of free government, the establishment of national unity, is far from fulfilled in most parts of the Middle East. With differing and often conflicting definitions of the nation, it is difficult to foresee the development of the strong ties which make possible the diversity within a common unity which is characteristic of free government.

Basic loyalties in most parts of the Middle East are still directed to the various religious groups, and divisions among them make it difficult to use those loyalties as the basis for the creation of a modern state. The Christian religious community is divided into Copts, Orthodox, Armenians, Catholics, and a handful of Protestants. Islam includes Shiites, Sunni, and the Druzes of Lebanon, while Saudi Arabia adheres to the Wahabi sect.

Each group is internally organized and self-conscious, which makes cooperation among them and the development of a national loyalty transcending religious differences almost impossible. Lebanon has succeeded in achieving a tenuous coexistence of the different religious groups in a political system organized on a confessional basis. Its parties are religiously based, and by agreement among the religious groups, it has a Maronite Christian president and a Muslim prime minister. The crisis of 1958, however, demonstrated that the system is able to survive only because of the efforts of a few able military leaders who have mediated confessional differences.

Although efforts have been made to develop a modernized state with an Islamic base, the strong traditional elements in Islam, and particularly the antiquated provisions of Islamic law, have made it difficult to forge national unity on this basis even in states that are overwhelmingly Muslim. Saudi Arabia, Libya, and, to a lesser extent, Morocco, have been able to use traditional religious loyalties in the service of the nation-state, but Nasser has had repeated difficulties with religious critics of his Arab socialism, and in Tunisia, Bourguiba has found that his efforts to abolish the annual Ramadam fast could not overcome the deep religious conservatism of the Tunisian people.

Islam has been able to adjust to a wide variety of political regimes, and it has achieved a *de facto* separation of church (mosque) and state for many centuries, but its doctrinal base has not been modernized to take account of the modern state in the way that Western Christianity, after much travail, was able to do. In orthodox Muslim theory, Islamic law and Islamic courts should rule over many aspects of social life. The nonbeliever should be governed by his own religious law, and the religious communities are to be kept separate. In the orthodox view, the only real nation is the nation of Islam.

Today the Islamic religion does not possess the political power it had when it knocked at the gates of Europe at Tours, in Spain, and at Vienna, but its legacy is a religious traditionalism and divisiveness which impedes the development of modern states in the Middle East.

The most successful nation-builder in the Middle East, Kemal Atatürk, felt that he would have to break the power of Islam if he was to succeed in creating a modern state in Turkey. Between 1919 and 1922, Kemal made a deliberate effort to destroy Islamic influence in Turkey. He changed to a Western alphabet from the Arabic, decreed the abolition of the fez and the veil, and abolished the caliphate to demonstrate the destruction of religious authority. He was only partially successful in his efforts at secularization, but his program produced one of the more modern states in the Middle East, and the modernizing military strong man became a model for other developing countries to imitate.

Kemal developed a doctrine of *étatism* to describe his policy of using the resources of the state to promote rapid economic development, thus anticipating the later programs of the nationalist leaders after World War II. He was largely successful in his policy of forging the nation of Turkey out of the ruins of the old Ottoman empire, but he viewed his role as basically a transitional one, preparing the way for a more modern constitutional parliamentarism. A few years after he had taken power, he encouraged the formation of an opposition party, and his successor, Ismet Inönü, actually turned over power to the opposition Democratic Party in 1950, when it won an electoral victory with promises to slow down the Kemalist policies of repression of Islam and state regulation of business.

The transfer of power to the opposition party would have been more encouraging if the Democrats had not brought on military intervention in 1960 by their persecution of their political opponents. The military rulers gradually transferred power back to the civilians, and there was a second victory for an opposition party in 1965, but the recent history of Turkey, like that of Lebanon, demonstrates that its democratic parliamentarism is still dependent on the benevolent cooperation and occasional intervention of the military.

The model of the modernizing military strong man has been further enhanced by the political success of Gamal Abdel Nasser in Egypt. In Turkey, democratic parliamentarism was established by Atatürk as an instrument of modernization in conscious imitation of Europe. In the case of Egypt, a parliament had been in existence since the last quarter of the nineteenth century, but it was tainted by corruption and under the direct or indirect control of the Turks or the British throughout most of that period. When the Free Officers dissolved the Egyptian parliament in 1952, and in the following year outlawed the middle-class nationalist Wafdist party as well as the Muslim Brotherhood and the Communists, few mourned the disappearance of Western-style democracy. While Nasser does not have the charismatic appeal of Kemal, he has succeeded in winning the loyalty and respect of the Egyptians and in projecting his image to the Arab world and to Africa as well. By a pragmatic and somewhat hesitant political evolution, he has adopted Pan-Arabism, Egyptian nationalism, and more recently a welfare-oriented Arab socialism as ideologies with a far greater emotional appeal than the liberal democratic formulas of the West.

If democracy is defined only as the involvement of the people, Nasser's regime is more democratic than those which preceded it, since many more Egyptians are now interested in and related to national politics than at any previous time. If, however, democracy means the existence of freedom of criticism and the possibility of legitimate opposition to the regime, Nasser's government is certainly not democratic. This is one of the reasons for the disagreement between Nasser and the Ba'thist or Socialist Resurrection Party in Jordan, Syria, and Iraq. This party shares many of Nasser's Pan-Arab and socialist goals, but it criticizes one-man rule and the suppression of opposition as contrary to the ideals of democracy.[1] The party is currently deeply divided, and its commitment to socialism and Arab nationalism is probably stronger than to free expression, but the party constitution strongly endorses free elections and freedom of association and expression.

In addition to the conflicting claims of traditional theocracy, the reforming military strongman, and liberal democratic parliamentarism, another institutional model—the nationalist single party—has been established in parts of the Arab world. In Tunisia, the Neo-Destour, now the Destourian Socialist Party, has provided a strong government under the leadership of Habib Bourguiba which seems to be responsive to the wants and needs of the population. In neighboring Algeria, a rather less personalistic Front of National Liberation has been in control, although since the overthrow of Ben Bella, the army leaders seem to

[1] See Munif al-Razzaz, "Parties—A Precondition of Freedom," in Paul E. Sigmund (ed.), *The Ideologies of the Developing Nations* (rev. ed.; New York: Frederick A. Praeger, 1967).

predominate over the party. Like the regime of the military strong man, the single party offers the possibility of the creation of national unity and development, although at the price of the suppression of some internal criticism and dissent. It also promises greater political participation in decision-making than does a highly centralized military regime. Its appeal is such that Nasser has repeatedly attempted to establish a government-sponsored single party in Egypt. In the early years of his regime, he created the Liberation Rally. From 1957 to 1961, this was succeeded by the National Union. Neither of these two organizations developed any mass support or grass-roots organization. The Arab Socialist Union, which has been in existence since 1962, has been somewhat more successful, but the Nasser regime is still basically controlled by the military officers who came to power in 1952.

Multiparty parliamentarism has been more successful in Israel than in the Arab countries of the Middle East. Frictions between the secular and the religious parties still exist; relations with the small Arab minority present a problem;[2] and the country is divided ethnically and culturally between the more advanced European and American Jews who established the state of Israel and those from the Middle East and North Africa who arrived subsequently. Nevertheless, Israel has been successful in forging a varied population into a nation and in creating a common consensus on democratic institutions which is lacking in the Arab world.

The reasons for this are not hard to find. The political elite in Israel is largely European in origin, outlook, and values. Israel is also a new nation, and except for the Arab minority numbering about 200,000 before the Israeli victories of June, 1967, it is religiously homogeneous and threatened by a common external enemy. Aside from a few religious traditionalists, it does not have to contend with forces hostile to the forging of a modern state found elsewhere in the Middle East.

Besides the religious divisions, the lack of a consensus on what

[2] The large Arab populations in areas occupied after the Israeli victory of June, 1967, are not represented in the Israeli parliament.

constitutes a nation, and the conflicting claims to political legitimacy, the Arab Middle East has other difficulties that impede the
development of democratic self-government. Many of them can
be related to the absence of the sense of individual responsibility
and initiative which has been discussed in earlier chapters. When
society is viewed principally in terms of religious and ethnic
groups, and the individual's primary loyalties are to families,
clans, and local religious communities, it is difficult to apply
liberal democratic norms to politics. Democratic self-government
assumes that at least some political decisions can be made by free
individuals acting alone or in concert with others. It is thus no
accident that the early democratic theorists in Europe derived
political obligation from a social contract made by the free
consent of equal individuals in the state of nature. It is difficult,
however, to transfer political institutions which have been based
upon a model of individual equality to societies in which the
primary unit is the group, deference is a virtue, and hierarchy a
fact of everyday economic and social life. Women have been fully
admitted to political participation only in the West in this
century, but the religious and customary barriers to participation
by women in politics in the Middle East are much greater.
Turkey has gone far in breaking down these barriers, and
Tunisia and Algeria have included women in their nationalist
movements, but the resistance to equality of the sexes throughout
the area of Islamic culture remains an obstacle to the full extension of political rights to all adult citizens implied by the theory
of democracy.

Literacy, as has been pointed out earlier, is an important aid
to the development of individual political participation and
criticism. It should therefore not be surprising that the Middle
Eastern countries with the highest literacy rates come closest to
attaining self-government. Israel leads the way with 84 per cent of
its population literate, while Lebanon is second with 70 per cent.
Turkey and Jordan have a 40 per cent literacy rate, and the
lowest rate (2.5 per cent) is found in Saudi Arabia.

It is true that political information in the Middle East has been aided by the widespread acquisition of transistor radios. However, the radio is largely a one-way communicator. Nasser's "Voice of the Arabs" stirs the listener to political indignation and action, but it does not offer him the same opportunity for intelligent reflection and discussion as the printed page. Television is also used as an instrument of political propaganda rather than of genuine political dialogue. The same charge may be leveled at much of the controlled press, but the possibilities for the presentation of alternative points of view are greater with a literate population that informs itself on public issues through newspapers and books than with illiterates who listen to speeches on transistor radios or watch them on television—if only because without the technical apparatus of a totalitarian state it is more difficult to control published materials.

Per capita GNP figures also provide some interesting evidence on the relation of economic development and democratic government. It is necessary, however, to omit oil sheikdoms such as Kuwait from consideration. (Kuwait, a tiny principality floating on a sea of oil, ranks first in the world in per capita GNP.) If this is done, Israel ranked first in the Middle East for 1957 with a figure of $726, twice that of the next Middle Eastern state, Lebanon, with a figure of $362. Much further down the list are Algeria and Syria with $178 and $173 respectively, followed by Iraq, Egypt, and Jordan.[3]

These figures do not prove an inevitable correlation between literacy or economic development and the existence of democratic government, but they tend to support the contention that it is easier for a people to develop a sense of individual independence, self-reliance, and free expression if they are able to read and write and possess a certain degree of economic independence, so that they can communicate their views.

The distribution of economic resources in the Middle East,

[3] See Bruce Russett *et al., World Handbook of Political and Social Indicators* (New Haven, Conn.: Yale University Press, 1964).

however, is such as to discourage hopes that economic development can bring with it progress toward free government. Oil is the principal source of income in the Middle East and most of it is concentrated in the most backward, relatively thinly populated areas of the Arabian Peninsula and the Persian Gulf. The United Arab Republic, with the largest population in the area (28 million), has only recently discovered oil, and it has very little else in the way of raw materials to promote economic growth. It also has the highest annual rate of population growth (3 per cent), so that whatever economic progress is made is barely able to keep abreast of the burgeoning population. Nasser's hopes for a great expansion in the Egyptian economy as a result of the completion of the Aswan High Dam seem doomed to disappointment unless further efforts are made to control the population explosion.

Since the time of Aristotle, the middle class has been regarded as the social group that provides support for constitutional democracy. In the Middle East, the economic basis for an independent middle class is lacking except in a few urban areas. In nationalizing the large and medium-sized businesses in the United Arab Republic, Nasser weakened the strongest middle-class group in the area, although he counterbalanced this by his attempt to create a class of rural small landholders through his agrarian reforms. Elsewhere the pattern is typically that of a polarization between a small upper class and poverty-stricken rural and urban masses. However, one writer on Middle Eastern politics has underscored the importance of the development of a bureaucratic middle group of civil servants and public officials which currently provides much of the more dynamic leadership in Middle Eastern politics.[4]

In the West, intellectuals played an important role in the development of democratic government. Such theorists as John Locke, Jean Jacques Rousseau, and John Stuart Mill provided

[4] Manfred Halpern, *The Politics of Social Change in the Middle East and North Africa* (Princeton, N.J.: Princeton University Press, 1963).

persuasive arguments for the development of democratic self-rule. After the middle of the nineteenth century, their arguments or those of their successors also appealed to the Europeanized Middle Eastern intellectuals. The ability of a nation to establish parliamentary government indicated to them that it had progressed along the road marked out by the advanced European countries. On this point, however, there has been a striking change since World War II. While liberal democracy still has its defenders among Middle Eastern intellectuals, the democratic ideal no longer has the universal appeal which it possessed in an earlier period. Most of the modernizing intellectuals are ready and even eager to lend their talents to a development-oriented authoritarianism. Viewing the parliamentarism of the past as a game played by upper- and middle-class professional politicians linked to foreign economic interests, they tend to see Western-style democracy as an obstacle to national development, at least in less developed countries. This change, which is part of a general rejection of Western models in many spheres of life, means that in addition to the many other obstacles to the establishment of free government in the Middle East, the lack of an educated leadership dedicated to democracy and free expression also makes unlikely a movement in the direction of genuine parliamentarism in the near future.

In view of the combination of the lack of ideological appeal, low literacy rate, economic problems, communal and segmented social structure, and inflexibility of religious traditions, it is easy to be pessimistic about the future of democracy in the Middle East. It is true that religious divisions may occasionally produce an internal balance which approximates that of democratic pluralism, as has been the case in Lebanon. It is also true that the rate of urbanization and political socialization has been increasing rapidly. A professional and bureaucratic middle class which is literate, politically conscious, and economically able to participate in politics is also developing in the major cities. Other signs of hope include the formation of the Arab Socialist

Union in the United Arab Republic, which may one day evolve into a genuinely democratic decision-making body, as well as the evolution of the Tunisian Destour Socialist Party, which often appears responsive to the wishes of student and trade-union groups affiliated with it. In Algeria, the army and the National Liberation Front have experimented with self-management committees in the nationalized factories and agricultural holdings, although the program has been de-emphasized recently. In Morocco, the king has developed a technique of consultation with political leaders, including those of the opposition, which has prevented serious disorder in a country divided between a well-organized urban proletariat and a traditional feudalism in the rural areas.

The Pan-Arab movement is less encouraging as a possible center for the development of pluralistic democracy. The principal Pan-Arab organization is the Arab League, which is a loose instrument of consultation principally directed against the existence of the state of Israel. It has been wracked by internal divisions between the radicals headed by Nasser and more recently the Syrians, and the conservative regimes in Jordan and Saudi Arabia. A feud between Nasser and Bourguiba has also divided the organization. For a time, when Egypt federated with Syria to form the United Arab Republic in 1958, it seemed that Nasser himself was heading an important Pan-Arab movement. However, within three years the Syrians withdrew, partly because of the personalism of Nasser's domination and partly because of his economic policies. Talks between the U.A.R. and Syria and Iraq concerning closer political links continue, but the rivalries between the states as well as economic, political, and personal differences have prevented the formation of common political institutions. Similarly in North Africa, the political and economic divergences between Morocco, Algeria, and Tunisia have prevented the creation of the proposed Maghreb Federation. Any effort to combine a monarchy, an army-dominated "revolutionary" regime, and a personalistic one-party state into a single political federation appears to be doomed at present.

When the political, social, economic, and religious factors obtaining in the Middle East are compared with those that influenced the rise of pluralistic liberal democracy in Europe and the United States, it becomes evident that the future development of the Middle East is unlikely to parallel that of the West. True, important changes—greater political participation by the masses, accelerated economic development and social reform, and a modernization of government, religion, and society—are taking place in that area, yet in terms of our earlier analysis, national unification has yet to be achieved in any real sense in most of the countries of the area. The values of individual freedom and independence are not strongly cherished and defended, and the social groups in most Middle Eastern societies have not yet attained that state of equilibrium of power within a basic consensus which enables the government to operate in consultation with, and by the consent of, most of its citizenry. The advances made in recent years have been principally under the auspices of authoritarian modernizing regimes with a commitment to welfare and economic development, but not to political democracy. Whether the changes which they have induced will ultimately bring about a political structure in which there is real consultation with the governed in an atmosphere of political freedom and protection of the rights of minorities will depend on a future evolution and historical contingencies which no one can foresee at this time.

8

LATIN AMERICA: DEMOCRACY
IMPOSED ON FEUDALISM

THE FUTURE OF DEMOCRATIC GOVERNMENT in Latin America is
obviously uncertain. A comparison of the political systems of the
American continent emphasizes this. In the northern part of the
hemisphere, two nations—the United States and Canada—both
products of Anglo-Saxon culture, enjoy stable democratic governments. To the south, the Latin American nations, products of the
culture of the Iberian Peninsula, seem to engage in a perpetual
alternation between democratic governments and dictatorships.
It would be wrong to define the difference purely in national-
cultural terms, yet it should be noted that the one part of the
hemisphere is the legatee of the entire history of Anglo-Saxon

democracy, while the other works out its destiny on the basis of political traditions and practices bequeathed to it by the Spanish and Portuguese imperial conquests of America beginning in the sixteenth century.

The birth of the multitude of nations in Latin America, none of which (with the possible exception of Brazil) is large enough to command a continental economy in the manner of the U.S.A., is clearly a consequence of the expansion of Iberian power to the area before the Industrial Revolution. No instruments of transportation and communication were available to construct a government able to exert its authority over a whole hemisphere. The fact that both Portugal and Spain were involved in the Latin American expansion of European power accounts for one basic division, the separate identity of Brazil. The other divisions have geographic and historical causes, such as the natural barriers of jungles and mountains, and the way in which the various independence movements modified the structure of the Spanish colonial empire.

But the weakness of democracy is caused not so much by the multiplicity of Latin American nations as by the one social fact that democratic institutions have been imposed on an essentially feudal hierarchical economic and social structure. In Europe, bourgeois democracy either destroyed feudalism or gradually transmuted it. In the United States, the feudal structure of the Southern cotton economy was so involved with the institution of slavery that its abolition in the Civil War destroyed Southern feudalism forever.

In Latin America, on the other hand, feudal inequalities and loyalties were exaggerated by the racial amalgam of Iberian conquerors and Indian natives. The natives became the patient peasants under the vexatious burdens laid upon them by their landlord conquerors. The Latin conquerors both enslaved the Indians and intermarried with them. At the time of independence, their mestizo—mixed blood—offspring outnumbered both the Indians and those considered to be "white" and formed a politically unstable intermediate group, estranged from the traditional Indian community but lacking the economic and political power of those of European racial extraction. Latin racial tolerance regarding racial mingling thus produced a less homogeneous pattern than the one produced by Anglo-Saxon racial intolerance, which consigned the native Indians to "reservations" while a purely Anglo-Saxon culture grew to power in North America.[1]

The Indian peasants were ignorant of the language of the conqueror and lacked both the cultural and technical competence to assert and defend their interests or to participate in the formation of a national spirit. Thus they were in the same condition of impotence as the European peasants had been earlier, before the craftsmen and the rising commercial classes organized their discontent and gave voice to their mute resentments.

The rise of the middle classes was postponed because Iberian culture was not touched by the winds of doctrine emanating from Renaissance and Reformation, which helped to dispel the contempt for both trade and manual toil that medieval culture had inherited from Aristotle, or at least had justified by his principles. Manual labor and mining were performed by the Indian hewers of wood and drawers of water. Trade was conducted by the mestizos, who suffered only a little less than the Indians from racial contempt. They certainly did not possess the social prestige and the self-respect to infuse the early national revolutionary movements with egalitarian political goals in the manner of the New England farmers and businessmen in the American Revolution. (Even in aristocratic Virginia, Jefferson voiced democratic sentiments in the name of the "husbandmen.")

As a result, the Latin American national revolutions at the

[1] It should be noted that there is no significant Indian population in Argentina, Chile, Uruguay, and Costa Rica. In these countries the Indians were either absorbed, placed on reservations (Chile and Argentina), or wiped out by disease and maltreatment.

beginning of the nineteenth century—inspired by the French Revolution and prompted by Napoleon's occupation of Spain— were only superficially "democratic." The French and American Revolutions influenced the political forms and slogans. Moreover, legitimacy derived from popular sovereignty was the only alternative for independent nations which had forsworn loyalty to a monarchical imperial system. But despite some efforts at social reform by leaders like Chile's Bernardo O'Higgins, democratizing influences did not reach down to the underlying social structure, which remained an unreconstructed feudalism.[2] In effect this meant that feudal lords and "caudillos" had the effective social power and used it in the exercise of their political power in the democratic assemblies. Democracy in these circumstances could not slowly transform feudalism. It became merely a superficial façade concealing the real power of the oligarchs.

To this day, even such nations as Argentina and Brazil, parts of which resemble our Western frontier in history, temperament, and social structure, have not shaken off the vestiges of a feudal economy and politics. Perhaps this accounts for the way in which both the Vargas dictatorship in Brazil and the Perón dictatorship in Argentina were able to build up powerful political machines by compounding military support and demagogic exploitation of the resentments of the workers and peasants against a "democratic" constitutionalism dominated by landed wealth.

If the new African nations are defective in the solidity of the national community from which their authority must be derived, most of the Latin American nations are defective in the possession of a tolerable equilibrium of social and economic power upon which the attainment of justice in free societies depends.

We have seen that in European democracies this equilibrium was tortuously achieved by the original development of strong middle-class forces and the subsequent development of the collec-

2 Feudalism is here used as a shorthand expression for a premodern hierarchical society in which political, economic, and military power were related to land tenure.

tive power of industrial workers. In Latin America, the feudal economic and social pattern has been so inflexible that in many cases the rise of industry accentuated the power of landed wealth but did not produce an independent middle class committed to democracy and freedom. The social structure in many parts of Latin America is dangerously akin to the situation in European nations at the beginning of the nineteenth century, and the plausibility of the Marxist indictment of bourgeois democracy is correspondingly strong.

It is easy to understand, therefore, why revolutionary Communism has a special appeal among Latin American students and intellectuals. Since, however, there is no immediate prospect of the type of total collapse of traditional institutions which took place in Russia and China, there is little chance of a wholesale Communist revolution in most of the nations of Latin America. However, the example of the Castro revolution in Cuba, in which a typical romantic Latin American revolutionary movement embraced Communism after coming to power and became a launching pad for Communist revolutionary activities throughout the hemisphere, demonstrates the fragility or the inadequacy of democratic institutions in the hemisphere. Castro has been able to support guerrilla movements in Venezuela, Colombia, Guatemala, and Bolivia in recent years, and to attempt to channel peasant discontent in the direction of the Communist movement. In Brazil before the 1964 military revolution, Communism also had some influence among the peasants, and the Peruvian land seizures in the early 1960's have likewise given evidence of the influence of organized Marxism.[3]

It is significant that the base for Communist activities in Latin America is principally in the rural areas and in the universities.

[3] It should be noted that the Communist movement in Latin America is currently divided into groups sympathetic either to Moscow, Peking, or Havana. Most of the Communist activity among the peasantry is carried on by Castroites, and it was on the grounds that it was an urban movement out of touch with rural discontent that Castro attacked the Venezuelan Communist Party in March, 1967.

The laboring classes where Marx expected the revolution to begin have given their support to other groups and movements. Only in Chile today and in Mexico and Guatemala in the past has there been significant Communist control of the labor unions. In Argentina, the workers are still under the spell of Perónism. In Brazil, the memory of Vargas is still strong, and his heirs controlled the labor movement until the 1964 military coup. In other countries, political parties such as the APRA in Peru and Acción Democratica in Venezuela possess strong labor organizations, and throughout the continent the Catholic trade unions organized in the Confederación Latinoamericana de Sindicatos Cristianos (CLASC) are gaining in strength.

Governments in power are able to win labor support by granting periodic wage increases which pass on some of the benefits from industrialization. Even Batista in Cuba was thus able to control the labor movement. Only the countryside has seen little or no improvement. There life remains as poor as ever, and dissatisfaction is on the increase. Modern commerce and industry under pressure from political leaders and from trade-union organizations will grant wage increases to the workers, but there is no effective way, short of a strong peasant union organization, to compel the landowners to pay adequate wages to the landless peasants. In the past, peasant dissatisfaction has supported non-Communist social revolutions in Mexico after 1910, and in Bolivia in 1952. In the future, however, it appears that the Latin American revolutionary trend may be monopolized by the Communists—if only because adherence to Communism assures the revolutionary of external support and a supply of arms. Peasant discontent thus poses one of the most serious threats to stability in Latin America, and because it can be and has been channelized in the direction of Communism, it can also be a threat to the development of democracy.

A further destabilizing element may develop out of the massive migration to the cities which has taken place in every Latin American country during the past fifteen years. In Argentina the phenomenon of Perónism demonstrates the dangers of a rapid expansion of the urban proletariat and its politicization by a demagogue. Thirteen years after his overthrow, support for Perón among workers and slum-dwellers is one of the principal factors impeding the development of stable democratic politics in that country. In other Latin American cities—in the *favelas* of Rio de Janeiro and São Paulo, the *callampas* of Santiago, the *barriadas* of Lima, and the *ranchos* of Caracas—hundreds of thousands of newly arrived slum-dwellers constitute an explosive potential, not so much at the moment—for they have not yet become a powerful political force—but in the future, as their children become politically aware and demand human dignity, political power, and a decent standard of living. (A similar generational difference has been noted among Negroes who have migrated from the rural South to the Northern cities of the United States since the end of World War II.)

In many countries of Latin America there is a highly developed modern sector which consciously imitates the United States and Europe and resents being classified with underdeveloped areas such as Africa, Asia, and the Middle East. The problem of Latin American development is how to extend the political and economic benefits of the modern sector to the newly awakening peasantry and slum-dwellers.

Of the four principal strategies which have emerged for dealing with rural and urban discontent, only one places any trust in democratic institutions. First, conservative military and civilian groups in such countries as Nicaragua, Honduras, Paraguay, and Haiti hope to maintain oligarchical control by a combination of force and persuasion, relying on centuries-old traditions of deference and apathy to restrain the pressures for social and economic change. Secondly, the military men in control in Argentina and Brazil and the technically oriented economists whom they support are promoting a program of economic development along classical lines, stabilizing wages and prices, and encouraging foreign investment while limiting free political activity in various ways. They argue that democracy can develop and new groups be incorporated only after a stable and prosperous economy has been established, and that political democracy must wait until the proper economic and social conditions are achieved.

In Venezuela, Colombia, Mexico, and Chile, democratic reformist governments have adopted a third position—positive action by the government to stimulate the economy, redistribute income, and incorporate the lower classes into the democratic process. With varying degrees of enthusiasm and success they are attempting to solve the pressing social and economic problems of their countries through political action and the utilization of democratic institutions.

This attempt has been rendered more difficult by the partisans of the fourth approach to social change, the revolutionary transformation of society along the lines of the Cuban model. Sometimes this partisanship is merely theoretical, and political competition is carried out within the democratic system, as in the case of the Communist and Socialist parties in Chile. More often it has taken the form of sporadic guerrilla activity in rural areas, occasionally combined with urban terrorism, as in Venezuela and Colombia.

At the present time, vigorous and often brutal action by the military establishments in the countries with guerrilla activity has lessened the likelihood of an imminent overthrow of the existing order. The death of Che Guevara and the destruction of the small guerrilla movement which he headed in Bolivia in 1967 seemed to demonstrate that the current prospects of success of guerrilla action along Cuban lines are not great. With American encouragement, "civic action" teams from the military have also attempted to win over the peasants with literacy, health, and welfare programs. In Venezuela, a democratic reformist government has defeated the strongest Communist guerrilla effort, and similar (but less successful) attempts are being made by President Méndez Montenegro of Guatemala, but the prospect for the future is that instability and violence in the rural areas will continue to threaten the weak democratic governments of Latin America so long as the peasant land hunger is not satisfied.

So long as the movements can be associated with Castro and Communism, the threat from the guerrillas has the ironic effect of reinforcing the power of the very social groups and practices against which it is revolting. The landowning classes can point to the specter of Communism and secure support in suppressing the legitimate demands of the peasants. The armed forces can get more American military aid and strengthen their domestic power and position if at last they have an enemy to fight. And if democratic governments do not make what in the view of the military is a sufficiently vigorous effort to suppress the unrest, the military can accuse them of pro-Communism and stage a *coup d'état*.

The leaders of the first Latin American nationalist revolutions were military men, and the tradition that the military should intervene to save the nation in times of peril has a long history in Latin America. Lacking a belief in the necessity of civilian supremacy, or strong social and political support for democratic leaders, many of the nations of Latin America have developed a historical pattern of alternating democratic governments and military dictatorships. Sometimes the military governments undertake needed social and economic reforms, but more often they simply preserve the *status quo* and expand the privileges of the military class.

For a time in the last decade it looked as if this pattern might be broken, as one after another of the military dictators lost power—Perón in Argentina, Rojas Pinilla in Colombia, Pérez Jiménez in Venezuela, and Odría in Peru. After a few years, however, a new wave of military takeovers swept through Central and South America, and there is no assurance that this will not continue in the future. Many of the military interventions in the 1960's, however, have been accompanied by promises of a swift return to civilian rule, and in such countries as Peru, Guatemala, and Ecuador, civilians replaced military rulers after the latter had seized power. (Alternatively, as in Nicaragua, El Salvador,

Honduras, and Bolivia, elections were held so as to give formal approval to military control.) [4] Yet the military still retains what it considers to be its right to intervene extraconstitutionally if the government is not conducted as it wishes (as recent coups in Peru and Panama indicate), and, in the cases of Argentina and Brazil, the military leaders have now decided to continue to hold political power for an indefinite period (although in the latter case limited political activity was permitted until late 1968).

In some cases, such as that of Brazil in 1964, military intervention saved the country from serious chaos and misrule, but the price has been the reinforcement of a tradition of military intervention which is not always exercised for the good of the country. The Dominican Republic and Argentina are two states which have yet to overcome the baleful legacy of the military dictators Trujillo and Perón. The case of Argentina also demonstrates that the habit of military intervention is easy to acquire and difficult to discard. For a period of seventy years before 1930, Argentine politics were carried out by civilians and in observance of the forms (although frequently not the substance) of constitutionalism. Then, in 1930, the economic crisis produced by the Depression induced General José Uriburu to intervene, and Argentina has been plagued by military coups ever since.

Yet by comparison with Africa and the Middle East, the democratic tradition is strong in Latin America. Influenced by the development of democracy in Europe and the United States, the democratic ideology commands a considerable degree of respect, and the belief in freedom of expression, an independent judiciary, and freely elected governments is still strong in theory if not in practice.[5] And in some Latin American countries, the

---

[4] The Bolivian case should be distinguished from takeovers in Central America, since President René Barrientos, although a military man, is a product of the 1952 revolution, claims to adhere to its reformist goals, and has an independent political base outside the military establishment in the Indian peasantry of the Cochabamba Valley.

[5] For an argument, however, that the partisans of democracy are merely one of many power contenders in the Latin American political process, see Charles W. Anderson, *Politics and Economic Change in Latin America* (Princeton, N.J.: Van Nostrand, 1967), chap. iv.

tradition of civilian supremacy over the military has become firmly established. Chile has not seen military intervention in its politics since 1931, and such interventions have been relatively rare throughout its history. Costa Rica has no standing army, only a civil guard. Most important, Mexico, which was plagued by disputes among its military leaders for several decades, has been able to establish the supremacy of the president and party for the past thirty-five years.

An earlier chapter mentioned the importance of the Judeo-Christian religious tradition in promoting the spirit of individual responsibility associated with democratic self-government. The Latin American area is to an overwhelming degree Catholic, at least nominally, but until recently its Catholicism has been that associated with the Counter Reformation, untouched by the reforms which have enabled Catholicism elsewhere to make a successful adjustment to the momentous changes in the modern world. Moreover, the Church authorities in the New World were closely controlled by the Spanish Government. In 1501, a Papal Bull granted the Spanish monarch the right to collect all ecclesiastical tithes with the understanding that he was responsible for the financial support of the Church, and in 1508, he received the right to nominate all higher Church authorities in the Spanish possessions. This meant that the Church in Latin America, or at least the higher clergy, encouraged submissiveness, deference, and passivity in regard to the civil authority, and although some of the lower clergy actively supported the wars of independence, the hierarchy generally sided with the Spanish monarchy. Ecclesiastical opposition to democratic currents was compounded by the anticlericalism associated with the French Revolution and adopted by many of the Latin American leaders of the early independence period. In the nineteenth century, the struggle over the relation of Church and State, and the specific issue of the fate of the Church lands, which were a principal source of its financial support, dominated the politics of many Latin American countries, and the Church was closely associated with the conservative classes and parties. Church influence was exerted to delay reform and has thus contributed to the development of the existing revolutionary situation in many Latin American countries.

More recently there has been a significant alteration in the attitude and conduct of the Church in Latin America. In recent years the hierarchy in countries such as Peru, Chile, and Brazil has recognized the need for social reform, especially in the field of land tenure. Church leaders have also broken the alliance with the conservative classes and supported reform movements such as the Christian trade unions, the rural syndicates in northeastern Brazil, and the Christian Democratic parties in many Latin American countries.

The rapid spread of the Christian Democratic party, which although not formally linked to the Church is based on Catholic principles of social justice as enunciated in papal encyclicals, is an encouraging sign of the changing role of Catholicism in Latin America. Drawing on the writings of the French philosopher Jacques Maritain, the Christian Democrats specifically derive the democratic form of government from Christian principles and accept the modern pluralistic secular state as the most desirable form of government. Applying the Thomist philosophical conception of the social function of property, they criticize the abuses of capitalism and support programs of agrarian reform, progressive taxation, and worker participation in management. Most successful in Chile, where in 1964 their presidential candidate, Eduardo Frei, received the largest plurality in Chilean history, the Christian Democrats have organized a network of schools, institutes, and auxiliary organizations (women, students, youth, trade unions) committed to democracy and social justice throughout Latin America. Ironically, however, their Catholic inspiration prevents the Christian Democrats from working with some important democratic groups whose anticlericalism is stronger than their passion for social reform.

The efforts at *aggiornamento* of the Church resulting from the Second Vatican Council have also been effective in changing the attitude of Church leaders toward democracy and social reform. Church lands have been redistributed, consumer cooperatives and workers' banks have been initiated under Church auspices, and social and political action encouraged. Not least of the renovating influences in the Latin American Church has been the large number of European and North American priests and religious who have been sent to Latin America to deal with the growing Latin American population.

The Roman Catholic Church in Latin America has not yet faced squarely the most serious economic and social problem in Latin America today—the population explosion. Parts of Latin America such as Costa Rica, the Dominican Republic, and Venezuela have the highest birth rates in the world, approaching 4 per cent a year. (In Latin America, only Uruguay and Argentina have relatively low birth rates.) While there have been a few statements by individual clerics in Latin America about the need for a change in Catholic doctrine prohibiting contraception, the traditional view has been supported by most of the hierarchy, especially since the papal encyclical on the subject in July, 1968. The effects of the high birth rate (and a correspondingly low death rate) can be seen in the squalid slums that ring every major Latin American city, and the pressure that this exerts on an already unstable political situation is unlikely to operate in favor of democracy and peaceful change.

The Protestant churches have been working with increasing success in Latin America, and the new spirit of ecumenism will make it easier for them to work in the future. There are about 7 million Protestants in a total population of 200 million in Latin America, and particularly large communities may be found in Brazil and Chile. Attempts have been made to draw a historical connection between Protestant individualism and the development of democracy, but this would not be applicable in Latin America, where Protestants are still a tiny minority, and some of the more actively proselytizing sects such as the Pentecostals are not known for encouraging the spirit of rationalism and individualism associated with the rise of democracy in Europe.

Literacy, as has been pointed out, is an important requirement for the development of a free society and free government. The Alliance for Progress has committed itself to a substantial investment in education, but literacy rates remain depressingly low in many parts of Latin America. The highest literacy rates are found in Argentina, Chile, and Uruguay, where 80–90 per cent of the population is literate. If accurate figures were available, we would probably find that Cuba under Castro also has a high literacy rate as a result of massive campaigns in the early part of this decade. The rate drops off sharply for countries like Brazil, where 60 per cent are literate, down to much lower figures for Nicaragua, the Dominican Republic, and Haiti. (In the last-named country, 92 per cent of the population is without primary education.)

The argument that literacy is an essential prerequisite to democratic government has been used to prevent illiterates from voting in several Latin American countries. At the present time, only literates can vote in Brazil, Chile, and Peru. In the case of Chile, which has a high literacy rate, this does not work any great injustice, but in the other countries it has the effect of excluding the most deprived groups from any means to secure peaceful redress of their grievances through the political process. On the other hand it can be argued that giving the vote to illiterates would only open the way to their exploitation by demagogues and dictators. In the case of Brazil, the decision of President Goulart to enfranchise the illiterates was one of the factors which contributed to his overthrow in 1964. (After the revolution, however, even the literate voters were partially disenfranchised by the withdrawal of political rights from many leading politicians and the establishment of indirect elections for the presidency.)

A review of literacy figures for Latin America seems to indicate that literacy aids but does not assure the survival of democratic government. The few Latin American countries with a long democratic tradition, Chile, Costa Rica, and Uruguay, all have high literacy rates. On the other hand, while Argentina has one of the highest literacy rates in the hemisphere, democratic government has had considerable difficulty there, and, in Cuba, Fidel Castro does not seem to think that a literacy program poses a threat to his authoritarian rule.

University students have been in the forefront of democratic movements throughout Latin American history, and one may hope that the expansion of enrollments in the Latin American universities might be accompanied by an increase in support for democracy. In many parts of Latin America, however, the university has become a principal center for the inculcation and organization of Cuban-inspired revolution, most notably Venezuela's Central University in Caracas, which has been one of the main sources of support for the guerrilla Armed Forces of National Liberation (FALN). On the other hand, an encouraging recent development has been the strength of the Christian Democratic movement in many Latin American universities and student movements.

For the students and intellectuals, whether Christian Democratic or Marxist (and these seem to be the dominant positions in the Latin American university) political liberalism as it developed in the West is frequently associated with economic liberalism of the Manchester variety, and the institutions of constitutional democracy are viewed as formalistic structures incapable of dealing with the basic economic and social problems of the hemisphere. "Socialism" and "revolution" have favorable connotations, while "liberalism" and "pragmatism" do not—and real democracy is understood to mean economic equality and social justice achieved by centralized government acting on behalf of the people, rather than the political pluralism, local autonomy, and constitutional restraints of the Anglo-Saxon tradition. There is thus an ideological problem in Latin American student attitudes toward democracy, since social and economic goals are given so much importance that the important political and institutional aspects of democratic government may be ignored and freedom sacrificed to economic development and social justice. (This is not to deny the importance of these two goals, nor the very real manipulation of democratic institutions by economic and social oligarchies in the past and present.)

The absence of a middle class in most of Africa and the Middle East has already been cited as one of the obstacles to the growth of free government there. In parts of Latin America, however, a vigorous and active middle class has emerged which has supported democratic reform movements such as the Christian Democrats in Chile, Romulo Betancourt's Acción Democratica in Venezuela, and José Figueres' Partido de Liberación Nacional in Costa Rica. Yet Argentina again seems to be the exception, since despite the existence of a large middle class, it has not been able to establish an effective democracy for the last thirty-five years. One writer has related this to the desire of a segmented, largely immigrant middle class to imitate the conduct and attitudes of the upper classes, while others assert that the middle groups favor military intervention to protect them from working-class (principally Perónist) demands for power.[6] There is thus no inevitable connection between membership in the middle class and support for democracy, although with the exception of Argentina and Brazil, the countries with the largest middle groups (Chile, Colombia, Uruguay, Costa Rica, and recently Venezuela) have tended to exhibit democratic political patterns.

It must also be admitted that in many Latin American countries the commitment to democracy on the part of commercial and entrepreneurial groups is a very limited one. When democratic governments attempt to engage in reform programs, they run into the combined opposition of the old landholding and the

---

6 See José Nun, "The Middle Class Military Coup," and Richard N. Adams, "Political Power and Social Structures," in Claudio Veliz (ed.), *The Politics of Conformity in Latin America* (New York: Oxford University Press, 1967).

new commercial classes, which block efforts at agrarian reform or tax legislation. Sometimes this is done within and through the democratic system itself, because the legislators share the attitudes of the conservative groups or are subject to economic pressures, while at other times a *coup d'état* may be necessary to prevent government restrictions of privilege.

Actions such as these by domestic and foreign business have confirmed the Marxist theories of capitalist exploitation, and restrictive practices and a lack of economic dynamism on the part of Latin American commercial and industrial elites have brought the system of competitive economic pluralism into discredit. Laws are passed providing for welfare programs and minimum wages for workers and peasants, but an inadequate government administration finds it impossible to enforce them. Industries are nationalized, but this is often followed by political featherbedding and inefficiency which costs the economy more than the earlier exploitative practices of private owners. (This need not always be the case. Pemex, the nationalized petroleum company of Mexico, after initial difficulties, has been operating efficiently and profitably in recent years. By contrast, the Argentine nationalized oil industry has been a failure and its national railroads an economic disaster.)

Are there no alternatives to inefficient socialism (whether nationalist- or Marxist-inspired) or a restrictive exploitative and foreign-dominated capitalism? The democratic-left parties of Latin America—both populist and Christian Democratic—and the supporters of the Alliance for Progress in the United States share the belief that government-sponsored reform can bring about changes in the present economic system that will promote democratic development and permit incorporation of previously excluded sectors of the population into the political process.

More enlightened and modern businessmen have also recognized the need for domestic reform and support the development of rural and urban self-help projects. Foreign businesses such as Sears Roebuck and Creole Petroleum are developing domestic entrepreneurship and training native business leaders in modern methods. The success of the Central American Common Market has helped to persuade Latin American leaders to announce a formal commitment to the establishment of a Latin American Common Market by 1985 which can overcome domestic restrictionism and promote a dynamic competitive system—a goal accepted by the presidents of the Americas at the Punta del Este Conference in April, 1967.

The Charter of Punta del Este, which established the Alliance for Progress in 1961, set as a target a per capita economic growth rate of 2.5 per cent annually. In actual fact, growth rates have varied from more than 5 per cent in Mexico, parts of Central America, and, until 1967, Peru, to an actual decline in economic growth in Uruguay and Argentina (not major beneficiaries of the Alliance). By expanding infrastructures such as communications, education, and transportation, the Alliance has assisted Latin America's economic development at a time when declining export prices for primary products indicated that it was facing imminent economic disaster. Economic growth, however, must be combined with social and political reform, and the Alliance for Progress has given dramatic support to projects for land reform, educational reform, and tax reform—and now to Latin American economic integration. In the first seven years of its existence, it has not produced any dramatic changes in Latin America, but it acts as a symbolic demonstration of American support for social and political change, and it provides an additional incentive for reform measures. Before the adoption of the Charter of Punta del Este of 1961, five countries had adopted agrarian-reform laws: Mexico after 1917, Guatemala in 1952 and 1956, Bolivia in 1953, Cuba in 1959, and Venezuela in 1960. Since the initiation of the Alliance for Progress, laws have been adopted in all of the other Latin American countries except Argentina and Uruguay.

Agrarian reform is not a panacea for the economic and political ills of Latin America, but if properly administered and supported, it can encourage the development of medium-sized landholdings which will be more economically productive than the old system of *latifundia* (very large landholdings) and *minifundia* (extremely small plots). Reform should also lead to the creation of a rural middle class which, it is hoped, will support moderate democratic government.

The critics of the current agrarian-reform laws point out that they may lead to a decline in production, that they often result only in windfall profits for landowners who sell unwanted land to the government (payment is usually partly in cash and partly in bonds), or that none of the existing laws go far enough in reorganizing land-tenure arrangements. In reply, those who have observed the Mexican and Venezuelan laws in operation point to the contribution which they have made to political stability and social peace. The Mexican *ejido* reform, which has involved communal ownership but individual farming of the land, has been less successful in increasing production than the more limited Venezuelan reform, which included provisions exempting highly efficient farms from expropriation. The two Chilean agrarian-reform laws are particularly designed to expand agricultural output and lessen Chile's dependence on imports for food. (However, unlike the Venezuelan law, the 1967 Chilean agrarian reform sets very strict upper limits on the size of landholdings.)

Tax reform is another central feature of the program of the Alliance for Progress. The taxation of income is a novelty in many Latin American countries, and the Alliance for Progress has assisted in devising methods of collecting and implementing new taxes. Tax laws are also being used to stimulate economic development and encourage reinvestment of profits in the domestic economy.

A lesser-known objective of the Alliance is a general effort to improve the productivity and efficiency of Latin American economic systems. Increased productivity and economic growth can produce tax revenues which can be used by governments with the will, the laws, and the administrative machinery to do so to expand welfare and education programs and improve the lot of the rural and urban masses. Without an expanding economy, no amount of social legislation can save democratic government from disaster. With dynamic growth and effective political leadership, social justice can be achieved, and this, more than anything else, can demonstrate the value of democratic institutions.

One effort to make democratic participation meaningful is the Popular Promotion program in Chile. This plan gives government support to the formation of neighborhood, community, and peasant organizations, which can act to involve the deprived classes in government and to express their grievances. (The adoption of a law in 1967 to encourage the formation of rural peasant unions is a particularly important part of this program.) By creating institutional structures through which formerly excluded groups can act, the program can help to bring about that equilibrium among social and economic groups and forces which we described earlier as a precondition for the attainment of a tolerable approach to social justice.

The same search for an equilibrium of power animates those pressing for a closer political union of the Latin American countries. The Organization of American States provides some of the advantages of political association, but it is flawed by the overwhelming military, economic, and political power of the United States, which in the opinion of many Latin Americans is able, because of its preponderant power, to make sure that the OAS carries out its wishes. The view expressed in the title of Juan José Arevalo's *The Shark and the Sardines* is obviously exaggerated (although the inaction of the OAS at the time of the CIA-supported invasion of his native Guatemala seemed to confirm his analysis), and recent studies of the OAS have demonstrated that it is frequently necessary for the United States to make major concessions in order to maintain hemispheric unity.[7] Nevertheless, the OAS and its related organizations seem to

[7] See C. Neale Ronning, *Law and Politics in Inter-American Diplomacy* (New York: John Wiley & Sons, 1963), p. 158; G. Connell-Smith, *The Inter-American System* (London: Oxford University Press, 1966), p. 322; and Jerome Slater, *The Organization of American States and United States Foreign Policy* (Columbus: Ohio State University Press, 1967).

assume a coincidence of U.S. and Latin American interests which may not always be present. Specifically in the case of the nationalization of American economic interests and the development of an independent foreign policy on such questions as relations with China, the potential exists for a conflict which would be less one-sided if there existed institutions in which the Latin Americans could develop a common policy.

In fact, they are already doing so within the OAS, as recent meetings on the reform of the OAS Charter have shown—although Latin American unity seems to center principally on the effort to secure a maximum of economic aid from the United States with a minimum of control on its use. The recently formed Latin American parliament also provides a forum for the promotion of common Latin American objectives.

One of the most important of these objectives for Latin American reformist parties and leaders is the extension and maintenance of democracy in the hemisphere. They do not share the conviction of the extreme left that the United States is the principal obstacle to the establishment of meaningful democracy in Latin America, but the history of U.S. intervention in the Caribbean area over the last three-quarters of a century is not an encouraging one.[8] Earlier it was aimed at gaining or ensuring strategic advantages (the Panama Canal) or enforcing the payment of debts, so as to remove pretexts for European intervention. In the postwar period, the United States has intervened directly or indirectly in the attempt to eliminate a real or supposed threat of Communism in the Caribbean.

The Communist threat has also been the reason for the program of military assistance to the Latin American republics under the Rio Treaty of 1947. While there is no doubt that this program increased U.S. influence on a crucial power factor in

[8] The United States has intervened militarily in Cuba (1898–1902, 1906–8, 1916–20, and through CIA support and training of Cuban exiles in 1961), the Dominican Republic (1904, 1912, 1916–24, and 1965), Panama (1908, 1912, 1918), Nicaragua (1909, 1912–33), Mexico (1914, 1916), Haiti (1915–34), and Guatemala (1954 through CIA aid to exile military groups).

Latin American politics, it is doubtful that it aided the spread of democracy. The resulting association of the United States with military dictators like Batista in the 1950's (aid to Batista was terminated in 1958, but by then the damage had been done) served to discredit American professions of support for liberal democracy throughout the hemisphere.

A realistic assessment of the effects of American influence in Latin America would qualify this critical appraisal by citing such examples as the enlightened conduct of the Roosevelt Administration at the time of the nationalization of the oil industry in Mexico in 1938, the financial support extended to the Bolivian revolutionary government after 1952 in what amounted to a subsidy of the nationalized tin-mining industry, or the political help given to the Betancourt reform administration in Venezuela after 1958. In the Kennedy era, the commitment to democratic government was made clearer through the recall of the U.S. Ambassador to Peru after the military coup of 1962, the support given to the short-lived Bosch regime in the Dominican Republic in 1962 and 1963, and the termination of military aid to Peru, Honduras, and the Dominican Republic following the overthrow of their democratic regimes. While this commitment has not been as clear under the Johnson Administration, chiefly because the Dominican intervention of 1965 was viewed by Latin Americans as antidemocratic in purpose and effects, it should be noted that the largest per capita U.S. economic assistance in the hemisphere has been going to the reformist Christian Democratic Government in Chile, and in 1966, U.S. pressure in Guatemala dissuaded the military from overthrowing the newly elected Méndez Montenegro regime. Similar pressure in Argentina, however, did not deter the military from overthrowing the democratically elected Illia government in June, 1966.

As the Argentine and Guatemalan examples indicate, in evaluating the U.S. role in Latin America it is necessary to distinguish between small weak powers or those heavily dependent on U.S. financial assistance and the larger, more independent states such as Brazil, Argentina, Mexico, and Peru, whose foreign and domestic policies are less subject to U.S. influence. Whether the U.S. desires democratic government or stable authoritarian regimes will have little influence on large nations whose political processes are primarily determined by domestic factors rather than foreign influences.[9]

A final judgment on the effect of the United States on the growth of democracy in Latin America must inevitably be a mixed one. Mixed, too, are the prospects for the future of free government in the area. A dynamic modern, commercial sector coexists and cooperates in many Latin American countries with backward traditional groups opposed to all change. Societies that are segmented along class, linguistic, racial, economic, and geographic lines find it difficult to establish the sense of national community and consensus within which democracy can develop. Traditions of revolution and *coup d'état* conflict with democratic standards of legitimacy. Now the submerged ethnic and economic groups are giving voice to their grievances, and the political and economic structures are having difficulty responding to them. Oligarchic control and military dictatorship is still a common pattern of Latin American politics and society. Even such giants as Argentina and Brazil have not been able to develop patterns of democratic stability and social justice.

Yet the picture is not completely dark. Social, economic, and political forces are producing a greater sense of national integration and political participation. An increasingly powerful middle class similar to its counterparts in Europe and the United States has emerged in the major cities of Latin America. Reform parties and an extraordinarily gifted group of democratic political leaders such as Raúl Leoni in Venezuela, Eduardo Frei in Chile, and Carlos Lleras Restrepo in Colombia hold out the hope that democracy has a future in Latin America.

---

[9] This conclusion is supported by a study of the alleged U.S. role in the 1964 military coup in Brazil in Thomas Skidmore, *Politics in Brazil* (New York: Oxford University Press, 1967), especially the appendix.

After years of political instability and chaos between 1910 and 1930, Mexico has developed a reasonably democratic system of government under the leadership of the dominant Party of Institutional Revolution (PRI), which with its system of sectoral organization is able to respond to the needs of the farmers, the workers, and the middle classes. It has carried out extensive redistribution of land, which has helped to create new economic groups. Education has expanded under government patronage, and a program of glorification of Indian culture has given the Mexican a sense of national pride. Economic development has been promoted by inviting foreign investment, while basic industries remained under national control and all businesses are staffed with Mexicans. The political and economic power of the Church has been broken, and after years of tension and persecution, a *modus vivendi* arrived at with the ecclesiastical authorities. Democratic institutions, civilian government, and comparatively free elections have achieved wide acceptance in the last thirty-five years, although recent student protests have revealed increasing dissatisfaction with the PRI monopoly of political power.

While the overwhelming majorities secured by the PRI make it difficult for opposition candidates to win (the right-wing PAN party occasionally wins local elections but the PRI dominates national politics), the processes of consultation that take place within the party every six years on the naming of the powerful but not re-eligible president seem to produce a quasi-democratic consensus candidate. There remain problems of student unrest, unemployment, and lack of opportunity for the poorest classes, but out of revolution Mexico seems to have achieved a tolerable combination of stability, democracy, and development.[10]

Uruguay has a much longer history of democracy, going back

[10] For more critical views of the Mexican system written from the perspectives of left and right, respectively, see Pablo Gonzalez Casanova, *La Democracia en México* (Mexico City: Ediciones ERA, 1965), and Frank Brandenburg, *The Making of Modern Mexico* (Englewood Cliffs, N.J.: Prentice-Hall, 1964).

to 1904 (except for a brief period in 1933) . During much of this period, it has been governed under an arrangement which assures the opposition the right to participate in government. The most recent example of this, the collegial executive adopted in 1952, has recently been abandoned in favor of a presidential regime in order to deal more effectively with the country's urgent economic problems. The change, however, has taken place by referendum, and the traditional democracy of "the Switzerland of Latin America" has been maintained despite considerable economic difficulties, although, currently, it is imperiled by its incapacity to deal with the uncontrolled inflation and the pressures of labor and student groups.

Democracy also has a long history in Chile. Military interventions in the 1920's and early 1930's mar a perfect record of successive democratic governments since 1891, at first under a parliamentary and later under a presidential regime. New social and economic groups have been successively incorporated into the political system throughout Chilean history. The commercial and merchant groups were able to challenge the power of the conservatives through the organization of the Liberal Party early in the nineteenth century. The middle and professional classes acquired a voice in the Radical Party organized in the middle of the century. Later, labor was represented by the Communist and Socialist parties, now organized in an electoral alliance, the FRAP. At present, the last unincorporated social group, the peasantry, is being organized by both the Communists and the Christian Democrats. Even with chronic inflation, considerable social unrest, and almost insoluble economic problems, democratic governments have been able to survive in Chile and initiate substantial reforms. The latest of these, the Christian Democratic Government of Eduardo Frei, has adopted a strong agrarian-reform law, made a mutually satisfactory arrangement for partial ownership of the American-owned copper mines, extended primary education to all Chileans, and promoted the participation of peasants and slum-dwellers in national life. Despite the fact that it faces strong opposition from both left and right, it has demonstrated that commitments to both democracy and development are not necessarily in contradiction in Latin America.

Costa Rica provides another example of democratic development in Latin America. While democracy has had an unbroken history only since 1949, the earlier politics of Costa Rica was generally more stable and democratic than that of any of its neighbors in Central America. In the last twenty years, power has been transferred in an orderly manner from one party to another, the military has been eliminated from national politics, education has continued to expand, and a program of welfare legislation and national economic development has been adopted. Despite one of the highest birth rates in the world, Costa Rica has been able to survive and prosper as a free society in a part of the world where such a political phenomenon is rare. Whether because of its class structure (a comparatively large middle class), economic characteristics (mostly medium-sized coffee farms), high literacy and education, or population composition (no racial minorities to speak of), Costa Ricans espouse ideals of national unity, democratic individualism, and social justice that provide the basis for a functioning democracy.

The recent history of two other Latin American nations— Venezuela and Colombia—is not discouraging for the prospects for democracy. In 1958, a military countercoup in Venezuela expelled the dictator Pérez Jiménez, and Romulo Betancourt was elected president of a reform regime. Betancourt survived threats from the Castroite left and the military right, and, in 1963–64, the first democratic succession in Venezuelan history took place when he turned power over to Raúl Leoni.

In Colombia, an agreement for an alternation of Liberals and Conservatives in the presidency during the period 1958–72 has brought a modicum of stability (although little reform) to a country torn by factional strife, rural violence, and social discontent.

"The coming explosion in Latin America" of which one

author wrote in 1963[11] has not yet arrived—and perhaps it never will. But those who cherish democracy and freedom are aware that there remain serious impediments to the development of genuinely prosperous and free societies in Latin America. Two of the most important countries of Latin America, Argentina and Brazil, seem far removed from attaining that goal, and others such as Haiti and some of the Central American countries appear to have little chance of attaining it in the foreseeable future. Even in countries with functioning representative institutions, constitutional democracy may become discredited by its incapacity to solve the problems of economic growth and social justice. Yet, the prospects for free government seem more favorable in Latin America than in most other parts of the less developed world, and, with the cooperation and support of the United States and determination on the part of Latin America's domestic leaders, there is hope for the political and economic future.

If the modernized sector can develop the political will and the economic surplus to bring the semifeudal and depressed areas into the national community through education, welfare, and reform, the impending crisis may be averted. If it does not, the rural areas and the downtrodden urban masses will rise up to destroy those who refuse them their economic and political rights.

[11] Gerald Clark, *The Coming Explosion in Latin America* (New York: David McKay, 1963).

9

ASIA: THE SUCCESS AND
FAILURE OF DEMOCRACY

THE SURVIVAL OF THE RELICS of ancient cultures and civilizations poses a particularly grave problem for the societies of Asia. They are struggling to cope with the demands of the modern world while retaining the deeply rooted traditional attitudes, loyalties, and practices which make it difficult for any government, let alone one based on democratic institutions, to assert and maintain its authority. It is difficult to generalize about an area as vast as contemporary Asia, but one can observe that traditional cultures and ways of life have a much longer history here than in Africa or Latin America. Ethnic, religious, and social divisions go much deeper, and they divide these societies into self-contained communities which the nationalist creed cannot easily bring together.

Parliamentary democracy, tried in many Asian states, has taken hold only in a few. Where it does exist, its survival has been problematic and erratic. The colonial legacy often included representative institutions, but they sometimes served only to reinforce the existing divisions in society or to provide politicians with a livelihood or an opportunity for corruption. Yet, with the great exception of China, most of the Asian states are working toward some type of intermediate system in which a large measure of authoritarianism is counterbalanced by various institutional or noninstitutional methods of expressing popular desires or grievances. In the absence of real popular participation and effective restraints on the rulers, they may not fit the definition of free government, but the new Asian systems may be fulfilling the essential requirements of maintaining order and responding at least minimally to the most serious needs and demands of their societies. Whether this can ultimately produce the delicate balance between consensus and cleavage which gave rise to free government in the West remains a question for the future.

In none of the Asian states do the obstacles to, and the opportunities for, the development of free government appear to be greater than in India. Centuries of foreign rule, overlapping cultural influences, and deep religious differences have produced a society with only the most tenuous common cultural base on which to build a sense of nationhood. British colonialism maintained and even reinforced some of these divisions through the use of indirect rule in the princely states and the encouragement of Muslim separatism at certain crucial points. But the British also developed a high-quality civil service staffed by Indians, trained an army which respects civilian authority, and evolved a series of representative institutions (under considerable pressure from the Indians, it must be said) which gave many Indian leaders experience in parliamentary government. The British presence also provided a common language in a country in which linguistic divisions have assumed major importance, and it promoted British ideals of liberty, self-government, and the rule of law.

These British legacies would not have survived any longer in India than they have in many African countries had it not been for the development of an organization and leadership able to provide the essential unifying symbolism and structure which ensured that India would remain a single country. The Indian National Congress, founded in 1885, and still the dominant political force in India, brought together all who desired an independent India. Its leaders, especially the charismatic Mahatma Gandhi, were committed to the maintenance of national unity and democratic government for India. Gandhi was able to infuse his philosophy of nonviolence into the movement and to maintain pressure on the British through fasts, demonstrations, and such mass movements as the Salt March of 1930. Successively in 1909, 1919, and 1935, the British extended Indian participation in government, and, when India attained self-government in 1947, its leadership had had long experience in dealing with the problems of the country.

Yet Gandhi and the Indian National Congress were never able wholly to overcome the deep communal divisions in India. The Muslim League fought for the creation of an independent Islamic state—Pakistan—and partition was effected at the time of independence, at a cost of millions of lives lost in communal rioting, and the creation of 12 million refugees. At the very moment of independence, Gandhi was assassinated by a Hindu communalist fanatic, and the mantle of leadership was taken over by his close associate and disciple Jawaharlal Nehru.

Under the leadership of Gandhi and Nehru, the Congress opposed the traditional caste system of India. The caste system, a relic of invasions thousands of years before and of a division of labor which had once been functional, divided India into four principal castes: the Brahmin, or priestly class; the Shatriya, or warriors; the Vaisyas, or merchants; and the Sudras, or workers.

In addition, there were more than 2,000 subcastes, and the untouchables comprised nearly 10 per cent of the population. Untouchability was officially outlawed after independence, and special arrangements were made to improve the lot of the members of the "scheduled castes," as they were then called, but the system remains a fact of social and political life in large areas of India today.[1]

Even with partition, about 10 per cent of the people of India remain Muslim, and they have been given political recognition by the election of a Muslim to the presidency in 1967. In addition, Christians, both Catholic and Protestant, form a small but influential minority. The Parsees exert strong influence in the business community of Bombay, and the Sikh variant of Hinduism is so important that it has recently forced the creation of a separate Sikh state in the Punjab.

Linguistic differences also have a political significance in India. Hindi was supposed to have become the national language fifteen years after independence, but opposition from the non–Hindi-speaking population of southern and eastern India has forced postponement of this step, and English remains the principal *lingua franca* among the Indian elite. Linguistic differences also led to rioting in Bombay a few years ago, and the state of which Bombay was a part was divided into two linguistically based new states.

Political differences were inherited from the British and presented one of the first problems of independent India. Agreements had to be negotiated with the various rulers of the former princely states to persuade them to give up their political power, and in one case, that of Hyderabad, an economic blockade and a military invasion were necessary. The continuing problem with Pakistan concerning Kashmir also dates from this period and has its roots in the fact that, at the time of independence, Kashmir's

[1] See Lloyd I. Rudolph and Susanne Hoeber Rudolph, *The Modernity of Tradition* (Chicago: University of Chicago Press, 1967) , Part I, "Traditional Structures and Modern Politics: Caste."

Hindu Prince acceded to India despite the opposition of a largely Muslim population that favored joining Pakistan.

The economic pattern of India at the time of independence was another source of division. India was and still is primarily an agricultural country, despite the size of its major cities, Bombay, Delhi, and Calcutta. Each village is a self-contained community with its own traditions and structures of authority which have little relation to the outside world. Kusum Nair, in her moving book about Indian villages, *Blossoms in the Dust,* describes a villager's answer to her question as to whether the people of the village had heard of the Congress. "Yes, we have heard of the Congress, but we are not sure whether it is a man or a woman." Studies like Mrs. Nair's of Indian villages have shown that the laws against untouchability and the government's efforts to introduce village self-government through the *panchayat,* or village council system, have had only a limited effect at the local level.

The government has attempted to deal with the divisions in India through the establishment of a secular state which transcends religious differences and through the creation of a federal system which can adjust to the local and regional differences in the country. More recently, the federal divisions have been redrawn to conform to the general pattern of linguistic differences. This effort has been marked by an attempt to tread the narrow path between, on the one hand, emphasizing subnational differences to the point where they threaten national unity and, on the other, suppressing legitimate differentiation to the point where rebellion becomes a likelihood. The federal system has allowed such potentially explosive legislative proposals as the proscription of the slaughter of cows and the prohibition of alcoholic beverages to be settled on a state level, but agitation by militant Hindu groups for national laws on these subjects continues.

With all its fissiparous and divisive tendencies, the Indian political system has been able to survive the vicissitudes of twenty years of independence without major changes or institutional breakdowns. Despite ethnic, religious, regional, economic, and social fragmentation, a sense of national unity has been maintained, and the Chinese attack in 1962, as well as the border war with Pakistan in 1964, has served to strengthen Indian nationalism.

The basic structure which maintains India as a nation, however, is the Congress Party. Particularly since the passing of the party's charismatic leader Jawaharlal Nehru, in 1964, India's future has depended on the strength of the party organization. An attempt has been made to capitalize on Nehru's personal popularity by electing his daughter Indira Gandhi as prime minister, but it is the party as a whole which must maintain the necessary dynamism and responsiveness in the political system of a nation which is also a subcontinent.

The party elite is made up of Indians who have been heavily subjected to the cultural influence and values of their former English rulers. These values have also permeated the Indian civil service and army. It is true that one important political leader, Kumaraswami Kamaraj (widely believed to have been the one responsible for the selection of Indira Gandhi as prime minister) does not speak English, but he is an exception. Whether the English political values will survive when a new generation takes over the leadership of the party, civil service, and army is an important question for all who are concerned about the future of free government in Asia.

Despite India's low level of literacy—about 30 per cent—and relatively moderate rate of economic growth, the leadership of the Congress Party has been able to maintain a functioning democracy as well as national unity. Economic interest groups, particularly the business community and the trade unions, have free access to the government. In the elections of 1952, 1957, 1962, and 1967, the various parties—designated by symbols such as the oxcart for the Congress Party and the sickle and corn ears for the Communists—competed under conditions of complete

political freedom. Since its opponents are divided, the Congress
Party has been able to maintain control of the national government throughout this period. Because of the single-member
constituency system, a popular vote averaging about 45 per cent
in favor of the Congress in 1952, 1957, and 1962 produced a
proportion of parliamentary seats held by the Congress Party in
excess of 70 per cent. In 1967, its popular vote dropped to 40
per cent, but the party managed to retain 55 per cent of the seats
in the lower house of Parliament. However, it lost control of nine
of the sixteen state governments and of the Delhi City Council. It
is still by far the largest single party, but its dominant influence
on Indian politics has been sharply reduced.

Support for the party has been gradually eroded over the years.
First the Communists were expelled; then the Socialists left.
More recently, a new right-wing group, the Swatantra (Freedom) Party has been able to capitalize on the continuing popularity of the hereditary princes who have given it support.
Further right-wing defections have created a People's Party, and
the Hindu communalists in the Jan Sangh Party who oppose the
secularism of the Congress platform have recently had considerable electoral success. (Jan Sangh tripled its congressional representation in the 1967 elections.)

The strength of the extreme parties at both ends of the
spectrum is increasing, and, as India's economic situation becomes critical, largely because of the nation's inability to provide
food for its expanding population, dissatisfaction with the government may lead to a period of political instability which could
threaten its democratic institutions. Already in 1959, the central
government and the Congress politicians reacted to the election
of a Communist government in the southern state of Kerala by
inducing the President of India to use his powers to take over
state governments when public order has broken down (in this
case, primarily because of rioting for which the Congress Party
was partially responsible) .

The Aid India Consortium is attempting to provide economic

assistance to carry India through a difficult period, and American surplus-food shipments have been crucial in this respect. New strains of wheat developed with American foundation support are beginning to increase agricultural productivity. If the economic problem can be solved, the basic strength of the political system should be able to preserve unity and democracy in India. It still will not have solved the problem of peaceful transfer of power to the opposition on a national level, but it will have maintained representative government and free expression. The very fact that free elections have been able to survive for so long has given the Indian people a sense of participation in, and loyalty to, the system, endowing it with a legitimacy that may strengthen it against potentially disruptive subnational loyalties. However, the forces of regionalism and religious, linguistic, and ideological division will continue to place a strain upon the structure of Indian constitutional democracy.

The Indian case demonstrates that, even when the factors of national unity, responsible individualism, and social equilibrium are not present to the same degree as in the political evolution of the West, a functioning democracy can be created, provided the commitment by the elite is strong enough, and a governing national party can provide stability and development.

The multiplicity of parties and the divisions within the country were among the factors contributing to the collapse of parliamentary democracy in Pakistan in 1958. After independence in 1947, the Muslim League broke down into contending factions and, in the face of the bickering and corruption of a divided political elite, President Iskander Mirza dissolved Parliament in October, 1958, and resigned his own office in favor of General Ayub Khan. Ayub has given Pakistan a relatively efficient and honest government, and he has also attempted to introduce a modified parliamentary system known as Basic Democracy, which he defends as being more appropriate for a country in which 85 per cent of the population is illiterate. Utilizing a system of indirect elections rising from the local area to the national scene, he replaced the Parliament with a National Assembly, elected through a hierarchical system of councils called Basic Democracies. In January, 1965, he legitimized his own rule by holding a presidential election in which he defeated Fatima Jinnah, the daughter of a former head of the Muslim League. Tensions remain between East and West Pakistan, which differ in culture and character (although they share the Muslim religion) and are separated by 1,000 miles of Indian territory. The problem of maintaining a balance between unity and diversity has not yet been solved in Pakistan, although the strong government provided by Ayub Khan, the link of a common religion, and the external threat of a larger and stronger India have been able to ward off chaos and secession. The form of government which has evolved under Ayub is not democratic in the Western sense. It outlawed parties until 1962 and has repeatedly proscribed and imprisoned leading politicians. However, an attempt has been made to involve the population in government, and Ayub rules in consultation with a legislature which is able to reflect popular opinion and, technically, even to vote him out of office (although this would be difficult to accomplish).

In contrast to the apparent lack of the preconditions of democratic government in India, there were many indications that representative government could survive and develop in Japan. Economic development began early in that country. After the Meiji ("enlightened government") restoration of imperial authority, in 1868, the influence of the feudal barons was destroyed by the modernizing elite, while loyalty to the emperor maintained national unity. Industrialization came quickly, perhaps too quickly, and, by a remarkable combination of government action and private initiative, Japan became one of the leading industrial nations of the world. Literacy rates have always been high, and technical skills were acquired rapidly. The first steps toward parliamentary government were taken in 1889, and a trade-union movement began to develop as early as 1912.

It would seem that, in terms of our earlier analysis, Japan

had most of the preconditions for the development of democratic government at a very early stage. But certain elements
were missing. Decision-making remained largely in the control of the *genro,* or elder statesmen, among the imperial ad-
visers, and it was they, rather than a bourgeois commercial
class, who stimulated and controlled the process of modernization.[2] The cabinet was responsible not to the legislature but to
the emperor. Agriculture continued to be in the hands of a small
landlord class, which rented its lands to tenant farmers at
exploitative rates, while the business sector was increasingly
dominated by a few large combines. The superficial attributes of
Westernization were imposed on a deferential social system
which did not encourage critical independence and self-reliance.
Above all, the military classes were not brought under the
control of the civilians, and they involved the country in a series
of expansionist wars—with Russia in 1905, with Germany in
World War I, in Manchuria in 1931, with China in 1937, and,
finally, with the Western powers in World War II. Resistance to
the military by the intellectuals and some political leaders was
eradicated by means of a program of political intimidation and
assassination, and the business and industrial elites supported
the military in the pursuit of the "Greater East Asia Co-pros-
perity Sphere" scheme. Economic development, industrialization,
literacy, and national unity led not to democracy but to aggres-
sive militaristic imperialism.

The American military occupation after World War II provided an opportunity for the establishment of new political
institutions, which, it was hoped, would promote the development of constitutional democracy. An authoritarian U.S. general,
Douglas MacArthur, decreed a series of far-reaching reforms
which did much to steer the Japanese economic and political life
in a direction more favorable to democracy. Wisely, it was
decided to retain the emperor as a symbol of continuity (after

2 See William W. Lockwood, *The Economic Development of Japan* (Princeton, N.J.: Princeton University Press, 1954) .

stripping him of his earlier claims to divinity), and, in his name, the occupying authority decreed a reform of the Japanese land-tenure system, which created a whole new class of middle-level property-holders and simultaneously greatly stimulated agricultural production. The economic combines known as the *zaibatsu* were broken up on the grounds that they had cooperated with the military leadership which had brought on the war. Trade-unionism was stimulated; the status of women was improved; textbooks were rewritten to emphasize democratic themes; and an attempt was made to impose a democratic constitution that renounced war and militarism.

Although most of the precedents for this type of imposed democracy seemed to indicate that it would fail, it had considerable success in Japan. With the same speed with which they had earlier adapted to industrialization, the Japanese took up the new democratic order and made it their own. Effective political parties developed; freedom of expression was encouraged; and a functioning parliamentary regime was installed. There have been occasional violent clashes in the parliament and demonstrations in the streets, but the basic norms of democratic parliamentarism have been adopted and implemented. The party system has evolved to the point where it approximates the two-party pattern, involving a right-wing Liberal Democratic Party and left-wing Socialists. (There are also other, smaller groups, including the new Clean Government Party and a small but influential Communist Party.) The trade unions and agricultural groups are large and well organized. Some of the economic combines which were broken up by the occupation authorities have been re-established, and a Self-defense Force has been created, but there is, at present, no prospect of the re-establishment of the prewar pattern of an expansionist industrial-military oligarchy.

An important reason for the basic soundness and stability of the Japanese political system is its high rate of economic growth. At an average annual growth rate of nearly 10 per cent in recent years, Japan has been one of the world leaders in economic development. Part of this is due to historical accidents such as the outbreak of the Korean War at a time when it could act as a stimulus to the re-establishment of Japanese industry, and part is due to sound economic action by a government which intervenes more strongly in the economy than it is willing to admit. In addition, the technical skill and high education of the Japanese population have contributed to its economic performance. An expanding economy has opened up opportunities for social mobility and has reduced political extremism so that the parliamentary system established after the war has been able to function without the strains other systems have had to undergo.

Yet, even with the favorable conditions of national unity, established parliamentary institutions, and emerging interest-group politics, one cannot say that the future of free government in Japan is secure. The opposition Socialist Party has marked out a political position which differs radically from that of the ruling Liberal Democrats. If the Socialists were to win an election and form a government, the transition in foreign and domestic policy would be a difficult one. Opposition groups have not been averse to resorting to rioting and violence, and the legitimacy of democratic institutions has not gone unchallenged. The Buddhist-influenced Clean Government Party, which has made major gains in recent elections, is also somewhat ambivalent about democratic institutions.

In social relations, the emphasis is still on group membership with primary loyalties directed to families and other small groups. The spirit of independence and individualism which was associated with the development of democratic government in Europe is less evident in Japanese life. Opposition is expressed in sometimes violent group action, and constructive rational discussion of public issues is difficult when the pattern of social interaction alternates between repression of differences and a strong emphasis on them. This is meant not to underestimate the real progress toward democratic government made by the Japanese during the last twenty years but only to note that, as elsewhere, these institutions rest on a fragile base even when many of the basic factors permitting or encouraging pluralistic democracy are present.

An external threat to Japanese democracy, the proximity and expansionism of China, seems less serious at the moment of this writing because of the internal upheavals and rivalries among the Chinese leadership. However, if a single leader emerges as successor to Mao Tse-tung and makes use of the increasing nuclear capacity of China to threaten its neighbors, Japan will be one of the first to feel the pressure.

One is less inclined today than in the past to see the triumph of Communism in China as the result of a kind of inevitable process of radicalization of nationalist revolution. As a result of the evolution of the politics of the newly independent countries in Africa, the Middle East, and Asia, it is now evident that Communism is only one of many alternative methods which can be adopted in developing and modernizing a traditional society. Some radical leaders such as Nasser, Sekou Touré, or the military leaders of Algeria have chosen a nationalist socialism which attempts to modernize and mobilize their societies without the social cost of a Communist revolution. Others have chosen one-party rule or constitutional democracy. Yet, the history of the Chinese nationalist movement shows that liberal democracy cannot be implanted overnight, as Sun Yat-sen wished to do, and that a military single-party regime must carry out social reforms and avoid bureaucracy, nepotism, and corruption or be overthrown by a radical or Communist group, as Chiang Kai-shek was overthrown by Mao Tse-tung.

The one country in which this process may be repeated is Vietnam. There, an early marriage between the forces of nationalism and Communism has given the Communist movement a vitality and popular appeal which it lacks in other parts of the world. One does not ignore the systematic campaigns of assassination and terrorism carried on by the Vietcong when one asserts that the Communist movement in Vietnam is large, well organized, and highly effective. It has also been aided by the ineffectiveness and divisions of the supporters of liberal democracy, as well as by the deliberate efforts of the French colonial authorities to prevent the development of an authentic middle-class nationalist movement. The attempt by the United States to assist in the development of a liberal regime in South Vietnam by supporting one of the few non-Communist leaders with legitimate nationalist credentials ended in failure when Ngo Dinh Diem became discredited as he systematically resorted to repression and authoritarianism to maintain his control.

In terms of our earlier analysis, one may ask what the prospects were and are for the development of parliamentary democracy in Vietnam even with the most well-intentioned and committed leadership. The divisions of Vietnam are not only political. The country is divided religiously among Catholics, Buddhists, and sects such as the Cao Dai, Binh Xuyen, and Hoa Hao; it is divided geographically between the residents of the fertile river valleys and the montagnards, or mountain-dwellers (this division is also ethnic) ; it is divided economically between sophisticated city-dwellers and rural peasantry. An almost classic case of the segmented society which is so common in underdeveloped countries, Vietnam has lacked a national leader other than Ho Chi Minh to invest it with a sense of basic unity. Even Ho does not seem to have the support of the majority of the population in the South, although his party has the organization and ruthlessness to suppress opposition, as it has done in the North.

Literacy figures are no more encouraging for Vietnam. Although the literacy rates have since been raised in both North and South, when the French left in 1954 the rate was below 20 per cent. The economies of both parts of Vietnam have been wrecked by the effects of the war, but even before escalation and bombing, per capita income was among the lowest in the world outside of Africa. It is true that South Vietnam had a slight export surplus of rice before the war, but today it is only because of American assistance that the South Vietnamese economy is able to survive. American pressure is also being exerted in favor of agrarian reform, but it is not easy to carry out a program of progressive social change in the midst of a war.

Those who are committed to majority rule and minority rights find it difficult to see how Vietnam can be governed democratically. A coalition of the representatives of various forces and groups is a possibility, but the Vietcong have given no indication of a willingness to participate in such an arrangement; yet, to exclude them would mean to continue the present conflict under the direction of a weak and divided leadership. The second alternative is a military government such as that which has been in control in Saigon, but U.S. support for such a government has compromised our claim to stand for democratic government throughout the world. (The elections of September, 1967, were not wholly successful in their attempt to lend a semblance of democratic legitimacy to the South Vietnamese Government, since candidates deemed Communist or neutralist by the military were stricken from the ballot.) The third alternative is to surrender to the superior organizational ability and nationalist appeal of the Communists, but this would probably mean turning the country over to a minority, with no guarantees of the participation (or even the basic human rights) of other long-standing groups in Vietnamese society. One can hope for a negotiated coalition government including the Vietcong or for a gradual transition to a genuinely representative, elected government, but the social structure, politics, and history of Vietnam do not offer cause for optimism.

Indonesia, despite its great wealth in mineral resources, exhibits the familiar pattern of overpopulation, religious and ethnic division, and a lack of preparation for self-government, making the prospects for political democracy seem very dim. Fifty-two million people of a total population of 78 million are concentrated on the central island of Java. The lion's share of the mineral wealth in oil, tin, and rubber, however, is located on the island of Sumatra. The population is principally Muslim, but there are large Christian and Buddhist minorities. The Dutch had restricted access to education, so that, in 1940, only 10 per cent of the people were literate, and only thirty-seven Indonesians had graduated from universities. Commerce rested largely in the hands of the Dutch and the Chinese, and, except for small numbers of civil servants, the Indonesian middle class was nonexistent.

The Indonesian constitution adopted in 1945 called for a bicameral legislature, and, although it was never formally implemented, President Sukarno governed in consultation with an appointed legislative body that included representatives of various religious and political groups including the Masjumi Islamic Party, the Christians, the Socialists, the Nationalists, and the Communists. In 1949, an agreement was reached with the Dutch by which an independent Federal Republic of Indonesia was formally recognized and elections were scheduled for 1950. Less than a year later, the federal structure was superseded by a unitary state with a single legislature, and the members of Parliament continued to be appointed rather than elected, until the first legislative elections, in 1955.

The legitimacy of President Sukarno's position was not derived from elections but from his role as leader of the nationalist revolution. He governed without having been elected, but, in the early years, he enjoyed strong popular support. Between 1950 and 1956, he was assisted by a vice-president, the Sumatran Mohammed Hatta, who had also been one of the leaders of the independence movement. Hatta's participation ensured the continuing cooperation of Sumatra with Java despite its divergent economic interest.

But, by late 1956, Sukarno had decided upon a different system of government, which he called "guided democracy," and Hatta resigned in protest. Rejecting what he called "free-fight liberalism, where half plus one is always right," Sukarno began to govern through an appointive cabinet in which all parties,

including the Communists, were represented. Arguing that the
Indonesian tradition called for government by consensus (*mu-
fakat*), he dissolved the parliament elected in 1955 and established in its place a much weaker appointive parliament, an advisory council, and a largely ceremonial People's Consultative
Congress representing occupational and interest groups in Indonesia. Shortly thereafter, he outlawed the Masjumi and Socialist parties and initiated a series of foreign-policy steps which
moved him into close collaboration with China.

The one group against which he did not dare to move was the
army. When the Communists, who had been receiving substantial support from the President, themselves attempted to move
against the army on October 1, 1965, the army reacted by initiat-
ing and encouraging a bloody purge of all who were suspected of
being Communists. A strong reaction against Sukarno ensued, in
which student demonstrations played a significant part, but the
army was careful to maintain the fiction of continuity in the
presidency while gradually stripping Sukarno of his power. In
March, 1967, he was finally replaced as president by General
Suharto. Indonesia today exhibits the familiar pattern of army
rule, modified by the participation of some of the more moderate
politicians, such as Hatta, who were not associated with Sukarno's policies. (The People's Consultative Congress and its
standing committee also play an important role.)

It is easy to blame Sukarno for the failure of representative
government in Indonesia, but there are other convincing reasons
why the creation of free government in this nation would be a
particularly hazardous enterprise. We have already mentioned
the colonial tradition of paternalism, the lack of a trained elite,
and the problem of regional differences. Other factors might also
be cited—and one way to illustrate their importance is to compare the Indonesian situation with that of India, which gained
its independence in the same period. India had a trained civil
service with a commitment to democratic government; Indonesia
did not. The Indian Army believed in civilian supremacy; the

Indonesian military did not stay out of politics. India proclaimed itself a secular state, but the preponderant strength of Islam in Indonesia posed a problem of relations with the Masjumi and other Islamic parties. The Indonesian parties were numerous, governing coalitions were shifting and fickle, and the financing of political activity was partly based on corruption. In India, a large single nationalist party, the Congress Party, has controlled the government since independence, and a federal structure has been able to take account of regional and ethnic differences, but, in Indonesia, an imposed unity has not been able to suppress regional differences and, in some cases, outright rebellion (as in Sumatra in 1958).

With less erratic leadership, a different development might have taken place, but, in terms of the factors listed above, the odds seem to favor some kind of authoritarianism with consultation, as in many other parts of Asia and Africa. It may be that Sukarno's mistake lay not in the form of government he devised, since the army is now governing in a similar fashion, but in the specific personal policies he pursued, ruining the domestic economy, alienating Indonesia from the rest of the world, and failing to provide the intelligent leadership his position required. The civilian-military coalition now in power seems no more inclined than he was to return to multiparty parliamentarism. Like him, it claims to be developing a specifically Indonesian style of consensus politics, although what it sees as the Indonesian consensus differs sharply from the policy of Sukarno.

The pattern Indonesia exhibits may be typical of the predominant form of government in the developing areas in the foreseeable future. Not wholly authoritarian, because it attempts to anticipate the desires of the people and to involve some of their representatives at least in an advisory capacity, it is certainly not wholly democratic, since the army, the party, the strong man, or the charismatic leader gives the national unity and decisiveness elected governments have been, on the whole, unable to provide. It is a fluid system, in which *coups d'état* sometimes perform the function of elections in keeping the government responsive to changes in opinion, if only that of a political elite. Each new government at least pays lip service to the value of democratic legitimacy. And as long as the more developed countries show that it is possible to combine efficient government and functioning democracy, the democratic ideal will remain as a standard, perhaps impossible of attainment for the moment (Do the Western democracies do more than approximate that ideal?) and a goal for a future which, let us hope, is not too far off.

At the same time, the efforts of the less developed countries to attain economic growth and social justice will serve to remind the more developed democracies that the mere forms of democratic institutions are not enough—that there is no reason for Western democracies to feel superior about their political system when they fail to share their wealth with the less fortunately placed peoples and when, in their own societies, meaningful political participation is often denied to groups because they are unable to attain the economic and educational levels at which they could participate actively in the democratic political process.

As the Western democracies increasingly recognize the need for government action to promote economic development and expand equality of opportunity, they are beginning to face the same problem that perplexes many developing countries—how to use the powers of government to create the economic and social conditions which foster meaningful democracy while maintaining the constitutional restraints and protections of individual freedom which have been such an important part of the liberal democratic heritage. The need to achieve a meaningful synthesis of the individual and collective aspects of the democratic ideal remains a continuing challenge to those who believe in democratic government now and in future years.

10

THE PROSPECTS FOR
DEMOCRACY: A REVIEW
OF THE LITERATURE

I N CLOSING, let us briefly compare the theories contained in this book with those of some other works on the same subject. We have emphasized three principal lessons to be drawn from the development of democracy in the West. First, free government cannot operate except within a commonly accepted geographical framework of the nation and a constitution or accepted institutions for making political decisions within that framework. Second, free government requires the participation of responsible individuals who believe in the ideals of free expression, protection of minorities, and participation in government. These are most likely to emerge where there is economic development, a relatively large middle class, and widespread literacy. Thirdly, restraint on government and the attainment of social justice are best assured when there exists a pluralism of interests which is enforced by an equilibrium of economic, social, and political power.

Aristotle was the first political thinker to speak of the conditions for a functioning democratic state. In Book IV, Chapter 11 of his *Politics,* he argued that the best practicable state, a moderate democracy with a low property qualification for voting, could only survive in a society in which the middle class was preponderant. In societies characterized by a polarization between the rich and the poor, he predicted that there would be an alternation between oligarchical government and mob rule. A more complicated version of the same theory appears in Chapter 2 of Seymour M. Lipset's *Political Man* (Garden City, N.Y.: Anchor Books, 1963), where it is argued that there is a positive correlation of a relatively high per capita income, urbanization, industrialization, education, a large middle class, and the maintenance of stable democracy. Our own analysis tends to emphasize the effects of these economic and social characteristics on the development of individualism and economic and social pluralism in a society. It adds the important prerequisite of national unity, which Lipset and Aristotle merely assume. As we have seen, this is not an assumption which can be taken for granted.

In a later work, *The First New Nation* (New York: Basic Books, 1963), Lipset corrected this omission and placed great emphasis on the need for the establishment of legitimacy and national unity as prerequisites for the development of democratic government. A similar approach using a different terminology is also taken by Dankwart A. Rustow in his recent book, *A World of Nations* (Washington, D.C.: Brookings Institution, 1967). In Rustow's analysis, the establishment of national identity and a recognized political authority must precede the effort to satisfy popular aspirations for political and economic equality.[1]

[1] Rustow is critical of the other parts of Lipset's theory, since he believes that education and economic development are an accompaniment or consequence of democratic government more often than they are a condition. See Rustow's "Democracy, Consensus, and the New States," in a forthcoming issue of *Government and Opposition.*

Yet, in the past, the establishment of viable nationhood has often taken place under antidemocratic auspices. Authoritarian monarchies created most of the modern national states in Europe, and more than a century ago, John Stuart Mill, writing on *Representative Government* (London, 1861, Chapter 4), recognized that unlimited monarchy is particularly suited to overcome "the spirit of locality" which represents an

> . . . obstacle to the progress of civilization which representative government would have had a decided tendency to aggravate. . . . It may be laid down as a political truth, that by irresponsible monarchy rather than by representative government can a multitude of insignificant political units be welded into a people, with common feelings of cohesion, power enough to protect itself against conquest or foreign aggression, and affairs sufficiently various and considerable of its own to occupy worthily and expand to fit proportions the social and political intelligence of the population.

A similar argument is used today by those who defend the use of authoritarian measures by the leaders of the new nations. But the revelations after the overthrow of Nkrumah as well as the "revisionist" writings mentioned in an earlier chapter have cast doubt on the thesis that authoritarian government is inevitable in the new nations or necessarily superior in the promotion of economic development and the maintenance of political stability to a system in which opposition rights are recognized. Our analysis, while recognizing the enormous obstacles in the way of the establishment and maintenance of democratic government in developing nations, gives examples of relatively democratic systems which have worked with tolerable efficiency and success in meeting problems of economic and political development (for instance, in Chile, Costa Rica, Uruguay, India, Malaysia, Ceylon, Israel, Turkey, Lebanon, and, in recent years, Venezuela and Sudan).

Effectiveness is a further condition for stable democracy cited by Lipset in *The First New Nation*. As he puts it, democratic government must provide a "pay-off" in the way of economic growth and rising living standards. Thus far, few of the new nations have exhibited high growth rates (the Ivory Coast, Israel, Taiwan, Mexico, and Iran are possible exceptions, while Japan is now classified as a developed country), but at least economic collapse has been avoided. The case of Nazi Germany amply demonstrates that the existence of a middle class, relatively high urbanization and education, as well as many other prerequisites do not automatically assure the continuation of democratic politics when a country's leaders prove incapable of dealing with serious economic problems. Other examples, already noted, where democracy has broken down in periods of economic crisis include Italy, Argentina, and Chile. If the strain of war contributes further to the economic breakdown, as in the case of the Kerensky regime in Russia in 1917, it is extremely difficult for a democratic regime to survive.

Our discussion of the relationship between the emergence of the middle class and the development of the ideals of free expression and democratic participation in the West may also be compared and contrasted with that of Karl Marx and Friedrich Engels. Part I of the *Communist Manifesto* observes that the economic advance of the bourgeoisie was accompanied by a parallel increase in their political influence as the communes and independent city-states of the Middle Ages were followed by the self-conscious third estate or commons of the parliamentary monarchies, and finally by modern representative democracy in which the bourgeoisie has "exclusive political sway." For Marx and Engels, however, "the executive of the modern state is but a committee for managing the common affairs of the whole bourgeoisie," and liberal constitutional democracy is only a façade masking the economic and political control of a narrowing circle of exploitative capitalists. They did not foresee that the middle class would increase in size and share its power with the previously excluded and exploited workers in such a way as to permit them, after much travail, to achieve their economic and political objectives without destroying the structure of representative government.

The class-analysis contained in Barrington Moore's *The Social Origins of Democracy and Dictatorship* (Boston: Beacon Press, 1966) both confirms and supplements the theories which we have outlined earlier. His explanation of the support for Fascism which came from commercial and middle groups in Germany and Japan reminds us that membership in these groups does not necessarily imply support for constitutional democracy—a point which we have also had occasion to discuss in our analysis of Latin America. In analyzing the differences between the conduct of the bourgeoisie in England and in Germany (with France somewhere between the two), Moore explains the support of the English bourgeoisie for representative government by referring to the strength of the commercial urban groups in England, their independence of the crown, and the early elimination of the peasantry as a potentially dissatisfied social group posing a threat to the social order. Moore shares with us an awareness of the central importance of the middle-class groups in the emergence of liberal democracy, but he places greater emphasis on agricultural changes and rural unrest than does our analysis (although once again, our discussion of Latin America, an area Moore does not consider, has some interesting parallels with his view).

A similar but broader view is taken by Lloyd Fallers in "Equality, Modernity, and Democracy in the New States," an essay in Clifford Geertz (ed.), *Old Societies and New States* (New York: Free Press of Glencoe, 1963). Fallers attempts to relate the political development of Europe, Turkey, India, and Africa to the form of social stratification from which each evolved —i.e., feudalism, bureaucratic empire, the caste system, and tribalism. In particular the feudal and caste structures are seen as more likely to produce the social equilibrium and decentralization on which democracy can build.

The problem with the Fallers theory is that while recognizing the importance of the starting point, it does not consider the important intervening steps before democracy emerged or was created. Thus feudalism was a common structural characteristic of most of Western Europe, but democracy only took root in certain countries and in all cases long after the collapse of the feudal order. In the case of African tribalism, the tribal structure of society has been linked variously with authoritarianism (Edward Shils, *The Political Development of New States* [The Hague: Mouton, 1962]), with one-party consensus government (Julius Nyerere, discussed in Chapter 6), and with constitutional limitations on power (K. A. Busia, *Africa in Search of Democracy* [New York: Frederick A. Praeger, 1967]). The centralized bureaucracy of the Ottoman empire also used the "mullet" system to deal with subject religious groups, and this segmented and divided Middle Eastern society almost as much as a tribal or feudal structure would have divided it. We may conclude that democracy can take root and flourish in many different social situations and that there is no single pattern of evolution of democratic government.

Our third precondition, pluralism of interests, somewhat resembles the thesis of William Kornhauser in *The Politics of Mass Society* (Glencoe, Ill.: The Free Press, 1959) although it attributes different causes and effects to it. Kornhauser, principally concerned with the ills of postindustrial democracy, argued that breakdowns in democracy in countries such as Germany and Italy after World War I, and its ineffectiveness in France and the Latin countries, were related to the lack in those countries of intermediate groups between the individual and the state. When the elites are in direct contact with the nonelites, says Kornhauser, they must either manipulate them through propaganda or become instruments of the emotions of the masses. The mediating intermediate groups channel and formulate the demands of the population while at the same time insulating the ruling elite from too intense and direct popular pressure. In our analysis the intermediate groups are also important in communicating with the government, but their principal function is to articulate group demands for social and economic justice.

In Chapter 3 of *Political Man,* Seymour Martin Lipset makes a further contribution to the discussion of intermediate groups by emphasizing the disirability of cross-cutting affiliations in moderating the intensity of political disputes. When individuals have loyalties to a number of intermediate groups which sometimes come into conflict, they develop a tolerance for divergence, and political differences become less intense than when each group has the total loyalty of its membership in the struggle for political advantage. (It need not be recalled that the latter is very often the case in the less developed countries, where primary groups and religious, tribal, or ethnic communities demand and receive total loyalty.) When differences are thus muted, it is possible to develop the cleavage and consensus that we have earlier noted as most conducive to the development of democratic government.[2]

Lipset supplements this analysis in Chapter 9 of *The First New Nation* with a discussion of party systems and their effects in moderating and accentuating cleavages in a political system. Here and in his discussion of cross-cutting affiliations he is evidently influenced by the work of Robert Dahl, a political scientist at Yale University, who has been working for many years and from a variety of perspectives on the question of the relation between divisions in a body politic and the persistence of democratic politics. Dahl has coined a new term, "polyarchy," to describe a political system in which alternative elites compete for voter support, and by which ordinary citizens control their leaders and are controlled by them. (See *A Preface to Democratic Theory* [Chicago: University of Chicago Press, 1956]). In an earlier work with Charles Lindblom *(Politics, Economics, and Welfare* [New York: Harper & Brothers, 1953]) he argued that a

---

[2] See also Rustow, *op. cit.,* for a discussion of geographical intermingling as a factor which promotes democratic conciliation to resolve differences (rather than civil war or secession).

considerable degree of social pluralism was necessary before polyarchal politics could emerge. More recently, his concern has been with the relation of political institutions to the expression and resolution of differences in society. In *Political Oppositions in Western Democracies* (New Haven, Conn.: Yale University Press, 1966) he analyzes "one of the greatest and most unexpected social discoveries that man has ever stumbled upon"— the existence of "an organized group within the political system to oppose, criticize, and, if possible, oust the leading officials of government" (pp. xvi and xiv). In his most recent book, *Pluralist Democracy in the United States* (Chicago: Rand McNally, 1967), he draws on much of his earlier work and attributes the success of American democracy to a combination of overlapping cleavages, ideological consensus, and the minimization of conflict through the political institutions of federalism, two-party politics, and the single-member, winner-take-all electoral system.

A belief that political institutions can ensure or at least assist in the promotion of democratic stability has characterized American thinking from *The Federalist* (No. 10) to the current Foreign Assistance Act (Title IX). While it is no longer assumed that the model of democratic government must include a two-party system or single-member district elections (Dahl recognizes that proportional representation and coalition government work well in societies with important ethnic or religious differences, and Sir Arthur Lewis in his *Politics in West Africa* recommends the system for use in the "plural societies" of Africa), political scientists continue to discuss which electoral and party systems are most useful in promoting compromise, consensus, and majority-building.

The degree to which institutions influence or merely reflect the underlying social, economic, and ideological realities is difficult to determine. In France, the recent establishment of the direct election of the president has encouraged a realignment of political parties, thus appearing to confirm the hypothesis of American political scientists that the presidential system has contributed to the persistence of the two-party pattern in American politics. On the other hand, it has also been argued that social and economic changes in France had already made the previous pattern of ideological politics obsolete.

Our own analysis has tended to look more to the ideological, social, and economic factors which contribute to the success or failure of democracy, since we consider that these are more fundamental than the specifics of democratic institutions. As the references to proportional representation indicate, political institutions must take account of the characteristics of the society for which they are designed, and no simple institutional transfer from one society to another is likely to succeed unless these realities are taken into account. Institutional variations are also necessary if the basic constitutional arrangements are to elicit the consent of the society for which they are intended.

There is considerable disagreement on the nature of the basic consent or consensus which is required for the operation of a successful democracy. Certainly all would agree on the need for common acceptance of the geographical boundaries of the political unit (our first condition) and the prerequisite of support for the institutions which mediate disagreement and produce political decisions. At the other extreme, there should be little quarrel with the assertion that a system which represses policy differences and places an overwhelming premium on complete consensus cannot really be called democratic. Edward Shils, in *The Political Development of the New States* (The Hague: Mouton, 1962), takes an intermediate position when he writes of the importance of "civility"—an implicit understanding by those in power of the limits of self-aggrandizement, a sense of self-restraint which does not abuse power either through corruption or the suppression of the opposition. Our own analysis places greater emphasis on the political, ideological, and economic pluralism which operates in favor of the development of this attitude—which is after all essentially a commitment to the democratic idea as well as to democratic institutions.

The existence of "a tradition of civility" may help to explain the continuation of democratic systems in countries such as Holland, Belgium, or Switzerland, where there are deep ideological, ethnic, and religious differences. Our analysis in the early part of this book has shown that some differences along economic, regional, and religious lines can aid in the development of the type of tolerance and conciliation of differences which characterizes democratic politics, but the second part of this book has demonstrated that if these differences go so deep as to make it impossible for the divergent groups to communicate or to use common institutions to resolve their differences, democratic government cannot operate. As Dahl has put it, "One perennial problem of opposition is that there is either too much or too little."[3]

Mention of toleration and a spirit of conciliation suggests the area of the psychological prerequisites of democracy. Our review of the development of democracy in the West has noted that the leaders of the democratic movement were characterized by a spirit of self-reliance and independence which encouraged them to demand participation in and restraint of government. Other writers have stressed different psychological characteristics as particularly conducive to democracy. John Stuart Mill, in the previously cited chapter of *Representative Government,* saw an excess of either "turbulence" or "passivity" as an obstacle to democracy (once again democratic government seems to require a middle position), and he attributed the instability of Latin American government to "the spirit of place-hunting" which attempts to exploit governmental power for personal profit. More recent studies on the relation of culture and personality to the emergence of democratic politics include Daniel Lerner, *The Passing of Traditional Society: Modernizing the Middle East* (Glencoe, Ill.: The Free Press, 1958) ; and Lucien Pye, *Politics, Personality, and Nation Building: Burma's Search for Identity* (New Haven, Conn.: Yale University Press, 1962) . Lerner con-

[3] Robert A. Dahl (ed.) , *Political Oppositions in Western Democracies* (New Haven, Conn.: Yale University Press, 1966) , p. 397.

siders the development of empathy and the capacity to adjust to
new environments and social change as requirements for political
participation on a national scale, while Pye discusses the identity
problems created by the conflicts between the socialization process
of traditional society and the demands of modern democratic
politics. A somewhat more complex model of psychological prerequisites for democracy appears in Gabriel Almond and Sydney
Verba, *The Civic Culture* (Boston: Little, Brown, 1965). In the
final chapter of that work, "The Civic Culture and Democratic
Stability," the two authors conclude that a stable democratic
politics requires a mixture of attitudes on the part of the citizen.
Primary social relationships must be characterized by confidence
and interpersonal trust, while broader political partisanship
should be tempered by a general emotional commitment to the
system as a whole combined with a pragmatic and instrumental
attitude towards the resolution of differences ("allegiant participant culture").

The Almond-Verba model notes that stable democracies also
retain considerable remnants of earlier types of "parochial" and
"subject" political cultures, and that these are necessary to a
functioning democracy, since if all aspects of human life were
politicized, too great a burden would be placed on the political
system and the individual citizen. We need not wait then until
all "place-hunting" has been given up, and all our citizens have
become empathetic and participant for democracy to develop—
and in fact, one may question whether these psychological ideals
have ever been attained in any political culture up to the
present.

Another contribution to the discussion of the psychological
conditions for free government is Harry Eckstein's "A Theory of
Stable Democracy," published as an appendix to his *Division and
Cohesion in Democracy, A Study of Norway* (Princeton, N.J.:
Princeton University Press, 1966). Eckstein develops a theory of
congruence of authority patterns to explain the stability of
democracy in certain countries and not in others. Beginning

from the assumption of a necessarily undemocratic pattern of authority in certain primary groups such as the family and the school, Eckstein argues that democratic government is best fostered when social authority patterns in intermediate groups tend to resemble those of government, in particular among those groups "adjacent to government." If there is a marked disparity of authority patterns between highly authoritarian private organizations and a highly democratic public authority, instability will result. On the other hand, an attempt to democratize all associations by fiat must fail, if only because some authoritarianism is necessary in all organizations and a considerable degree is necessary on the primary level.

Eckstein's theory resembles the one which we have developed, although there are also important differences. In our discussion of the development of individualism we emphasize the causes of the emergence of the free responsible individual, while Eckstein looks for its effect, a pattern of democratic participation in decision-making. Like Eckstein, we are also concerned with intermediate groups, but we look to their economic causes and political effects rather than their internal authority patterns. And in view of the analysis given in the preceding chapters of this book we must agree with Eckstein's conclusion that "stable democracy is immensely difficult to achieve, and has in fact been achieved only in very few cases—that it is unstable democracy, not stable democracy, which is, by any reasonable measurement, the 'normal' case" (p. 285).

Unstable democracy is the normal case because the democratic idea still has great appeal, and when the authoritarians fail, as they so often do, the only legitimate alternative is to be found in democratic institutions. The discussion of the geographical, economic, social, institutional, and psychological preconditions of democracy often underestimates the intrinsic power of the democratic idea itself. Free government may have arisen in a particular era in a particular part of the world, but the ideals which it embodies have a broader appeal. It also has received powerful confirmation from the example of the success of democratic systems in coping with problems of economic and social change. Conversely, a reverse demonstration effect can take place when Western democracies fail to live up to their professions of freedom, democracy, and equality, either domestically or internationally.

The prognosis for the future of democracy in the developing areas is a mixed one. Sometimes the circumstances will be such that a democratic leader and a particular combination of historical accidents will permit these forms to take root and grow. In many more cases, once the pattern of traditional rule is broken, a cycle of alternation of democracy and dictatorship ensues for reasons we have outlined above. And sometimes, as in Communist states, a combination of ideology and organization permits the authoritarian pattern to continue unbroken (although not uninfluenced by the popular will). The prospects then are for continued instability in a world in which stable, efficient democratic government is an ideal more often than it is an operative reality.

INDEX

192 *Index*